Indian Pilgrims

Critical Issues in Indigenous Studies

Jeffrey P. Shepherd and Myla Vicenti Carpio
SERIES EDITORS

MICHELLE M. JACOB

Indian Pilgrims

Indigenous Journeys of Activism and
Healing with Saint Kateri Tekakwitha

THE UNIVERSITY OF
ARIZONA PRESS
TUCSON

All author royalties are being donated directly to the National Tekakwitha Conference to support their ongoing efforts to strengthen culture and spirituality among Indigenous peoples. By purchasing this book, you are supporting an Indigenous-led nonprofit organization. Kw'ałanuúshamash! (I am grateful to you!)

The University of Arizona Press
www.uapress.arizona.edu

ISBN-13: 978-0-8165-3356-5 (cloth)
ISBN-13: 978-0-8165-3965-9 (paper)

Cover design by Nicole Hayward
Cover illustration: *Creation Turtle* © Pendleton Woolen Mills

Publication of this book is made possible in part by the proceeds of a permanent endowment created with the assistance of a Challenge Grant from the National Endowment for the Humanities, a federal agency.

Library of Congress Cataloging-in-Publication Data
Names: Jacob, Michelle M., 1977– author.
Title: Indian pilgrims : indigenous journeys of activism and healing with Saint Kateri Tekakwitha / Michelle M. Jacob.
Other titles: Critical issues in indigenous studies.
Description: Tucson : The University of Arizona Press, 2016. | Series: Critical issues in indigenous studies | Includes bibliographical references and index.
Identifiers: LCCN 2016007487 | ISBN 9780816533565 (cloth : alk. paper)
Subjects: LCSH: Indians of North America—Religion. | Indians of North America—Ethnic identity. | Tekakwitha, Kateri, Saint, 1656–1680. | Feminist spirituality. | Indian women activists. | Spirituality—Catholic Church.
Classification: LCC E98.R3 J25 2016 | DDC 299.7—dc23 LC record available at https://lccn.loc.gov/2016007487

Printed in the United States of America
♾ This paper meets the requirements of ANSI/NISO Z39.48-1992 (Permanence of Paper).

Contents

Illustrations

Acknowledgments

I am blessed to know and work with so many great people. Most of all, I have the most wonderful family, who model love and community in powerful ways: Mom, Dad, Uncle Jim, Roger, Gina, Justin, Alicia, Garret, Hunter, Faith, Quintic, Hazen, Blaise, Sealy, Chris, John, Karen, Dean, Gloria.

Special thanks to the National Tekakwitha Conference, whose attendees and staff were absolutely wonderful and inspiring before, during, and after the major research for this project. Thank you for your kindness!

Thank you to my advisors over the years, and especially the mentors who helped me develop my writing and author's voice: Sharon Elise, Garry Rolison, Kristin Bates, Beth Schneider, Kum-Kum Bhavnani, Laury Oaks, Inés Talamantez.

Christopher Andersen, Theresa Jacob, Jennifer Goett, and Karen Leong read early drafts of my work and provided incredible feedback and encouragement—thank you!

Students in my University of San Diego Gender in Native America and American Indian Health and Spirituality classes were helpful in our many discussions about the importance of Kateri Tekakwitha.

Many thanks to my University of San Diego College of Arts and Sciences deans, Mary Boyd and Noelle Norton, both of whom provided Faculty Research Grant support for this project.

Special thanks to all my University of San Diego departmental colleagues, who provided an inspiring place to do my work: Chair Jesse Mills, Alberto Pulido, Gail Perez, May Fu, Josen Diaz. I am so proud of the community vision we established within USD Ethnic Studies. Big thanks to Esther Aguilar, who provided essential and excellent administrative support, kept our department on track, and assisted with the final formatting of this manuscript.

Thank you to my Ethnic Studies 332 students, who organized the first Water Walk at USD in the spring of 2015. Special thanks to the students who provided helpful feedback on the discussion questions at the end of the book: Courtney Atienza, Nick Bihr, Courtney Burke, Celine Castillo, Jessika Duran, Nick Hoin, Cassandra Huinquez, Hanna Jugo.

Thanks to my colleagues at the Center for Native Health and Culture at Heritage University on the Yakama Reservation, especially Julia Silberman and Lupe Jimenez-Rios. Melissa McCoy and Jessica Black are tremendous colleagues who powerfully shape the vision and accomplishments of the Center. We founded the Center with support and commitment from Heritage president John Bassett.

A special thank-you to my mom, who provided the greatest inspiration to finish this book, through innumerable gestures of support and love, including asking, "Are you still working on a book about Kateri?"

Thanks to my longtime Faculty Success Program buddies, especially Jennifer Goett, for phone calls that helped keep me on track, and Lorraine Cordeiro for her kindness and strength. Kerry Ann Rockquemore's mentorship has had lasting effects—thank you!

Thanks to mentor Morgan Giddings, who reminded me to embrace abundance as I worked through the last stages of writing.

Special thanks to Leonora Siminovis-Brown, who spent hours in solidarity with me, encouraging me to finish edits. Incredible thanks to these fabulous colleagues who have been so supportive of my work, and who offered kindness and inspiration at key moments: Angie Morrill, LaShaune Johnson, Ethel Nicdao, Belinda Lum, Joana Jansen, Janne Underriner, Kelly Gonzales, Gayle

Skawen:nio Morse, Leisy Abrego, Molly Talcott, Dana Collins, Sylvanna Falcón, Dian Million, Maile Arvin, Andy Smith, Chris Finley, Polly Olsen, Rex Quaempts, Robin John, Mary James, Perse Hooper, Tom Reifer, Karen Teel, Lisa Nunn, Judy Liu, Chris Nayve, Jeffrey Burns, Dwight Lomayesva, Joely Proudfit, Mary Jo Poole, Nicole Guidotti-Hernández. Virginia Beavert encouraged me to write about Saint Kateri, and I'm grateful for her words of advice over the years.

I want to give special thanks to all the people who are featured in this book, through their powerful images, interview quotations, and forms of activism. Each person helps us onto a path toward the Cycle of Healing. Together, we are working toward decolonization.

I am grateful to Allyson Carter for placing my work in excellent hands. Special thanks to the anonymous reviewers who gave careful and thoughtful feedback. Thanks to Sheila Wilensky for her skillful copyediting and kindness. Huge thanks to Myla Vicenti Carpio and Jeff Shepherd for conceptualizing and leading important scholarly efforts, such as their Critical Issues in Indigenous Studies series. It is an honor to be included in this series.

Finally, an extra big thank-you to my blessed camping buddies, Chris and Anahúy. Áwna!

Indian Pilgrims

1

Indian Pilgrims Honor Their Native "Sister"

Ethnographic Introduction: Rising Before Dawn for a Spiritual Journey

*L*ike their ancestors before them, several American Indians awoke early, *before sunrise, to prepare themselves for a spiritual journey. They splashed water on their faces and gave thanks to the Creator for the new day, a blessed day for which they had long awaited. Some of them paused to reflect on the ones who could not be there on the journey, due to illness, frailty, or death, and knew that representing them on the journey was an honorable responsibility. After their morning reflections and prayers, they carefully dressed in regalia and gathered the materials needed for their journey. Some brought eagle feathers, some wore sacred medallions, others wore moccasins or jewelry passed down in their families through generations. In this way, they carried on a tradition that has been taking place in Indigenous communities for countless generations: preparing for and embarking on a sacred spiritual journey to honor the Creator, one's ancestors, and to pray for the well-being of oneself and one's community.*

What made these spiritual journeyers different, perhaps, was that they would not vision quest in the forests, valleys, or deserts of their Indigenous

Figure 1 Indian Pilgrims gather at dawn in Saint Peter's Square in Vatican City on the morning of Kateri Tekakwitha's canonization. Credit: Michelle M. Jacob.

homelands, nor would they attend a ceremony in their community's longhouse. Rather, they would load themselves onto tour busses and take a short drive from their modern Roman hotels to Vatican City. Over 800 American Indians had traveled thousands of miles from their homelands in the United States and Canada, and would witness the warm autumn sun rising and reflecting gloriously off the rich façade of Saint Peter's Basilica. They were excited for the climax of their spiritual journey, when they would witness and experience the spiritual transformation of Kateri Tekakwitha, a humble Mohawk/Algonquin young woman, into Saint Kateri Tekakwitha, the highest honor for a human being within the Roman Catholic Church. While we stood waiting to be allowed into the seating area for the canonization ceremony, I marveled at the diversity of Indigenous peoples surrounding me in the waiting area. We were there together on a pilgrimage to honor a holy Indigenous woman, and then it occurred to me: We were Indian Pilgrims.

Kateri Tekakwitha and the Cycle of Healing

Kateri Tekakwitha* is the first North American Indian saint canonized by the Roman Catholic Church. Her devotees have advocated for her sainthood since her death in 1680. In this book, I examine Saint Kateri's influence and relation to three important topics: caring for the environment, building community, and reclaiming the Native feminine as sacred. The narratives surrounding Saint Kateri are fascinating and, at times, contradictory. In my analysis, I examine Saint Kateri as a strong Indigenous woman figure who inspires diverse peoples to strengthen their spiritual commitments. It is perhaps ironic that this work, which celebrates Indigenous peoples, cultures, and women, takes place within the deeply patriarchal and settler colonial context of the Roman Catholic Church.

Many of the Indian Pilgrims I mention in the opening ethnographic note to this chapter are members of the National Tekakwitha Conference, an Indigenous-led nonprofit Catholic organization. The primary work of the National Tekakwitha Conference is to organize, in collaboration with different Indigenous communities, a national conference to bring its membership together. A different Indigenous community hosts this national conference each summer, bringing hundreds of Kateri devotees together from across the United States and Canada. Each day, they pray for Kateri's intercession to help their prayers be answered. Conference activities include workshops on cultural and religious topics, keynote speakers, communal meals, social powwow dancing, a healing and reconciliation service, and daily Mass. Several Kateri devotees report that the Indigenous woman has interceded to bring about miracles in their lives. Previous to Saint Kateri's canonization in 2012, conference attendees regularly prayed that the Vatican would elevate the Indigenous woman to sainthood. Now that Kateri is a saint, the

---

*In my research, I found that Kateri Tekakwitha's devotees most often refer to her as "Kateri," although some say "Saint Kateri" and some refer to her as "Tekakwitha." I use each of these names in my writing to honor the Indigenous communities' various preferences for naming this holy woman.

conference attendees continue to gather and pray together as a community of people who are devoted to the holy Indigenous woman.

Some of the work and history of the National Tekakwitha Conference has been documented by Mark Thiel and Christopher Vecsey's edited volume, *Native Footsteps* (2012). *Indian Pilgrims* builds upon the work of Thiel and Vecsey, whose edited collection of Catholic writings and Indigenous oral histories about Saint Kateri Tekakwitha was published by Marquette University Press with support from the Bureau of Catholic Indian Missions. In their volume, Mark Thiel (archivist of Native Catholic collections at Marquette) and Christopher Vecsey (professor of humanities, Native American studies, and religion) are the first to publish a collection of narratives from an oral history project (Thiel and Vecsey 2012). In *Indian Pilgrims* I extend this work by analyzing the cultural, political, and social significance of Saint Kateri within contemporary Indigenous communities from a critical Indigenous studies perspective. I analyze Saint Kateri's importance with regard to Indigenous cultural teachings about spiritual responsibilities to care for the environment, build community, and work toward gender justice, a concept that is central in Native feminist analyses. The theme of spiritual responsibility is woven throughout the book, as spirituality is a central feature of Indigenous cultural teachings—it is not separated from other realms of life but is indeed woven into all other realms (Fur 2002, Deloria 2003).

My work applies a decolonizing and Native feminist approach as I articulate the importance of centering Native women in my analysis, with the goal to envision pathways forward that will help to decolonize our social institutions (Smith 2005b, Arvin, Tuck, and Morrill 2013). As such, this book is a contribution to two growing fields within Indigenous studies: decolonization studies and Native feminisms. As a Native feminist analysis, *Indian Pilgrims* is concerned with gender justice, which is a process of respecting the autonomy of women and encouraging collectivist thinking and strategizing, while working toward collective remedies that challenge the colonial and capitalist status quo (Smith 2008, 161). All peoples benefit from gender justice, as it promotes a more equal and collectivist way of being—for our lives, our communities, our institutions, and our society. In *Indian Pilgrims*, I build upon my previous work of examining principles of Native feminism "on the ground" in Indigenous communities, and our people's struggles for decolonization and healing (Jacob 2008, 2010b, 2013). I articulate the importance of grassroots activism for theory building within Indigenous communities, and argue that Saint Kateri is at the heart of an Indigenous social movement that serves as a model for those working to honor Indigenous peoples and cultures *within* Western institutions.

In my analysis, I articulate the Cycle of Destruction and Cycle of Healing taking place within Indigenous communities and the Catholic Church. I illustrate the two cycles below in figures 2 and 3. Within the Cycle of Destruction, colonial logics of Indigenous inferiority are used to justify the dispossession of Indigenous homeland and the eradication of Indigenous cultures and languages. Often framed as a mission of benevolence (from a colonizing Catholic perspective), the cycle is, in fact, deeply traumatizing for all peoples (Native and non-Native) involved, and dismissive of Indigenous perspectives and accounts that contest the colonial logics and the destructive cycle. Yet, Indigenous peoples and allies have a long history of resisting the powerful Cycle of Destruction, reframing historical encounters, reclaiming Indigenous cultural traditions, and decolonizing the past, present, and future (Smith 2012). As Dian Million articulates, the witnessing and testimony of Indigenous peoples serve as resistance to the Cycle of Destruction (Million 2009, 2013, 2014). Indigenous peoples, who engage in healing through storytelling and activism, perpetuate a Cycle of Healing. Rather than rejecting Indigenous cultural traditions, Indigenous peoples reclaim their Indigenous cultures and languages, and use Saint Kateri Tekakwitha as an inspiration of the narratives of Indigenous cultural pride and worthiness. This rearticulation of mission reclaims Kateri as a strong Indigenous woman figure who is rooted in her culture, and special *because* of her connection to Indigenous peoples, not *despite* it (Palmer 2014, Bonaparte 2009).

The Cycle of Healing demonstrates Indigenous empowerment and the centrality of Saint Kateri as a figure who helps Indigenous peoples decolonize their minds, spiritualities, and lives. The Cycle of Healing helps to show us a pathway forward toward what Tink Tinker describes as "more powerfully healing theologies" (Tinker 2014). Throughout Indigenous communities, Saint Kateri provides inspiration for Indigenous Catholics and non-Indigenous peoples too. At the canonization event there were many non-Indigenous people who had a serious devotion to Saint Kateri, noting that

Cycle of Destruction

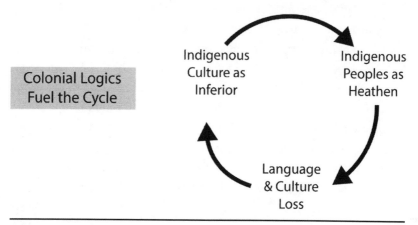

Colonial Logics Fuel the Cycle

Indigenous Culture as Inferior → Indigenous Peoples as Heathen → Language & Culture Loss →

Figure 2 Cycle of Destruction. Credit: Michelle M. Jacob and Christopher J. Andersen.

Cycle of Healing

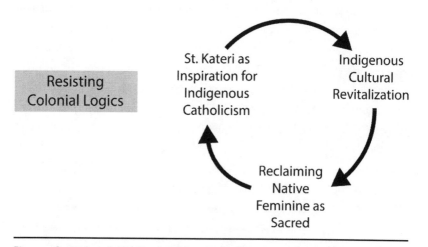

Resisting Colonial Logics

St. Kateri as Inspiration for Indigenous Catholicism → Indigenous Cultural Revitalization → Reclaiming Native Feminine as Sacred →

Figure 3 Cycle of Healing. Credit: Michelle M. Jacob and Christopher J. Andersen.

she inspired them, helped them, and that they felt compelled to make the long journey to Rome to honor her. Saint Kateri inspires all of her devotees to acknowledge the wisdom of Indigenous cultural traditions and reaffirm the importance of Native women as sacred beings. As Indigenous elders have stated, Saint Kateri's power does not reside in an official proclamation by the Vatican; she was "a saint already" in the minds of many of her devotees, before the Roman Catholic Church canonized Kateri in 2012 (Clairmont 2012, 145).

The Cycle of Healing does not derive its power from the Catholic Church's decision to canonize Saint Kateri. Rather, the Cycle of Healing is powerful because Indigenous peoples lead the cycle by drawing from their own cultural traditions to heal the wounds of colonialism. *Indian Pilgrims* shares several examples of the Cycle of Healing in action. Saint Kateri is an important symbol to inform my analysis of Indigenous-led movements to protect Mother Earth, build community, and reclaim the Native feminine as sacred. Healing is needed for us to all attain a "Good Mind," which Vera Palmer describes as being highly valued in Mohawk and Iroquoian cultures. Mohawk scholar Taiaiake Alfred describes the Mohawk concept, Kaiwiio, as being a Good Mind that is central to Indigenous resurgence and survival (Alfred 2005). Thus, a Good Mind has, from a Mohawk perspective, a philosophical and political meaning that informs balance and powerful reasoning (Alfred 2005). Palmer defines a Good Mind as being "a mind unburdened by the destructive effects of unmourned loss and bitterness, a disposition set upon honoring kinship bonds, despite temporal loss" (Palmer 2014, 287). Palmer describes how Kateri Tekakwitha's saintly qualities were due to her understanding of traditional Iroquoian culture, and the evidence that she had a Good Mind. We can all strive toward having a Good Mind as we enter into and perpetuate a Cycle of Healing.

Contestations and Contradictions

Throughout *Indian Pilgrims*, we will examine contestations and contradictions that surround Saint Kateri. For example, while Kateri, a Mohawk and Algonquin woman who lived in the 1600s, represents a powerful Indigenous woman figure to Kateri devotees, she is also portrayed by historical Jesuit accounts as leaving her "heathen" people to live among French Jesuits, so that she could dedicate her life to Jesus Christ. From the beginning, the Catholic Church narratives about Kateri situated Indigenous peoples at the bottom of a racial hierarchy, and in doing so further justified the "Manifest Destiny" that fueled colonial policies, which dispossessed Native peoples and waged a cultural and physical genocide, even as colonists and missionaries sought support for their work of saving Indigenous "heathen" souls (Newcomb 2008). It is important to analyze such colonial logics and their historical and contemporary meanings and complexities. These colonial logics fueled the Cycle of Destruction. Yet, Indigenous peoples and allies have contested these logics, pointing out that Kateri Tekakwitha lived among Indigenous peoples in New France, forming a close friendship with another woman with whom she proposed to start a new religious order for Native women. Additionally, the narratives about Tekakwitha rarely discuss how her Mohawk village was devastated by disease and war, both examples of the chaos and violence that colonialism brought to her people. Part of what makes Kateri Tekakwitha so interesting is the fact that she means so many different things to different peoples. Over the past three hundred years, Saint Kateri has become the most visible representation of Native American Catholicism.

Indigenous studies scholars have persuasively argued that representation is very important to Indigenous peoples, especially within Western institutions. Oftentimes the goal is not simply to be "included" in mainstream Western institutions, but to transform institutions through a radical process of indigenization (Mihesuah and Wilson 2004). Historically, Indigenous peoples have been brutalized and colonized by Western "progress" promoted throughout dominant institutions, including religion (Deloria 1992). Yet, master narratives of history often fail to tell the many ways in which marginalized peoples "speak back" to power. Kateri Tekakwitha represents a powerful figure who, in many Indigenous peoples' perspectives, transforms Catholicism and provides Indigenous peoples and their allies with meaningful ways to center Indigenous culture within their spiritual practices. It is a strong example of both/and analysis that disrupts essentializing dichotomies, which feminist scholars have critiqued (Collins 2000). Not content to be squeezed into a narrow box of authenticity (Collins 1998) as either "Catholic" or "Indigenous," Kateri devotees seek to combine Indigenous and Catholic traditions in a way that transforms their spiritual lives to have greater meaning. I argue that this process of indigenizing the Catholic Church is a form of decolonization, defined by Wilson and Yellow Bird as "the intelligent, calculated, and active resistance to the forces of colonialism that perpetuate the subjugation and/or exploitation of our minds, bodies, and lands, and . . . is engaged for the ultimate purpose of overturning the colonial structure and realizing Indigenous liberation" (Wilson and Yellow Bird 2005, 5). Through their decolonizing practice, Kateri devotees are engaging in resistance against the Cycle of Destruction that reclaims the importance of Indigenous womanhood and strengthens the culture and traditions of Indigenous peoples.

Data and Methodology

My project is a multisite ethnography. I traveled to Italy and Vatican City for the canonization event in October 2012 to do ethnographic fieldwork. I took photos, conducted interviews, and gathered print materials about the canonization event. Additionally, in April 2013 I traveled to Kateri's homeland and conducted a focus group with Mohawk women on the Akwesasne Reservation, which is located in upstate New York, southern Ontario, and southern Quebec. Finally, I collected data at community events on my home reservation (Yakama) and the National Tekakwitha Conferences in El Paso, Texas (2013); Fargo, North Dakota (2014); and Alexandria, Louisiana (2015); at these conferences I conducted ethnographic fieldwork as a participant-observer and conducted qualitative interviews. Appendix 3 contains the interview guide I used. All interviews were audio recorded and transcribed verbatim, then coded for themes using a grounded theory approach (Strauss and Corbin 1990, McGhee, Marland et al. 2007). In chapter 5, I reflect upon my teaching about Saint Kateri in my classroom, and I highlight student responses in 2015.

My researcher subjectivity was important in this process (Brayboy and Deyhle 2000). I am an Indigenous woman, a tribal member of the Yakama Nation in Washington State, and was raised in the Catholic Church.

Through networks of Indigenous scholars and activists, I recognized several people at the canonization, several of whom I have known for my entire life. During my three years of research and fieldwork, I strengthened and maintained old and new relationships alike. This approach of attending to the importance of relationality, being accountable to one's communities, is a main point of Indigenous epistemologies; Indigenous studies scholar Shawn Wilson states, "An Indigenous research paradigm is relational and maintains relational accountability" (Wilson 2008, 70). Wilson connects the Indigenous tradition of storytelling with contemporary endeavors of research: "Accountability is built into the relationships that are formed in storytelling within an oral tradition. As a storyteller, I am responsible with whom I share information, as well as ensuring that it is shared in an appropriate way, at the right place and time. In receiving the story, you as an active listener are responsible for putting the story into a relational context that makes sense for you and for listening with an open heart and open mind" (Wilson 2008, 126). I apply Wilson's framework in *Indian Pilgrims* by centering Indigenous voices and perspectives in my analyses. I share these stories with you, the reader, with the hope that they offer you ideas for entering into and perpetuating a Cycle of Healing.

Saint Kateri is popular on many Indian reservations, including my home reservation (Yakama). According to a study by Georgetown University, 18.3 percent of American Indians/Alaska Natives are Catholic (Gray, Gautier, and Gaunt 2014). The Bureau of Catholic Indian Missions serves reservations across the United States, including Yakama. I am a social scientist who engages in research on decolonization and Native feminism. I am interested in questions of Indigenous subjectivities and empowerment. These personal and professional realities shape my approach to the project.

In addition to my fieldwork, qualitative interviews, and focus-group data, I also draw from Catholic Church accounts of Kateri's life, including her biography written by Francis X. Weiser, a Jesuit priest who was concerned with "presenting the life story of Kateri . . . the most famous and heroic girl of the great nation of the Iroquois" (Weiser 1971, 11). I draw from these diverse data to investigate the inherent contradictions within Kateri narratives and examine the ways in which her story and representation can help people make sense of the intersection of religion, race/ethnicity, and gender.

Kateri Tekakwitha's Identity and Representation

As a social, cultural, and historical figure, Kateri refuses to have a simple and unified fixed meaning. Similar to many other issues across Native America, meanings of identity, spirituality, and history are not fixed (Jolivétte 2006). One powerful visual example of the contradictions surrounding Kateri is her large portrait that was mounted outside of Saint Peter's Basilica as part of the canonization. While attendees rejoiced that a Native woman's image was being honored in such a prominent way, some attendees questioned whether the image erased Kateri's indigeneity; the portrait, painted by a French Jesuit, Father Claude Chauchetière, circa 1696, portrayed Kateri in the likeness of a nun cloaked in a habit.

In contrast to the Vatican-sanctioned image, Tekakwitha's devotees brought other representations of Kateri with them to the canonization. These other images portrayed Kateri in markedly different ways, including visible markers of diverse regional indigeneity such as braids, a fringed shawl, jewelry, and buckskin regalia, as shown in the banner in figure 5. One woman, Marlene McCauley, carried this banner from Phoenix, Arizona, to the Mass of Thanksgiving, which took place inside of Saint Peter's Basilica on the day after Kateri's canonization. In the banner, Kateri is surrounded by nature, including evergreen trees, honoring her homeland in what is now upstate New York, and lily flowers, which represent Kateri's virginity. The banner proudly proclaims that Kateri is more than a mere saint; she is the "Princess" of the holy Eucharist, indicating her special place as honored royalty in God's Kingdom. This bold statement is made on a piece of vinyl that traveled from the United States to Rome, then to the inside of the Vatican, the headquarters of one of the most powerful colonizing forces on Indigenous peoples. It is a transnational message that proclaims a proud Indigenous identity, yet is heavy with Catholic overtones.

While the banner shown in figure 5 upholds Catholic themes, and prominently features the cross, I argue that the simple act of displaying this alternative image of Kateri represents a resistance to the master narrative of Catholicism within Indigenous people's lives. Rather than merely accepting the Church's representation of the Indian saint, Tekakwitha's devotees

Figure 4 Image of Saint Kateri as portrayed by the Vatican at the canonization event in 2012. Credit: Michelle M. Jacob.

Figure 5 Banner of Saint Kateri, proclaiming she is the princess of the Eucharist.
Credit: Michelle M. Jacob.

traveled thousands of miles, many wearing their traditional regalia, and showed another image of Kateri, one that is thoroughly Indigenous.

Indigenous peoples also honor Kateri by wearing jewelry that features Kateri's image. One Yakama woman at the canonization, Kateri Craig (named after Kateri Tekakwitha), wore a beaded necklace that featured a Kateri prayer card in the middle of the necklace. In this representation, Kateri's holiness is indicated by the illumination around her; she is perhaps in prayer because of her focus gazing off into the heavens with her hands folded softly below her heart. She again has two braids and is wearing buckskin regalia, marking her indigeneity in a way that is popular among contemporary Native Americans. The cross is featured, but it is a lesser focus than the holy woman's face. See figure 6. While clearly Saint Kateri is the feature of the necklace, the impressive beadwork around Kateri's image also projects a strong Indigenous identity and representation. The elaborately beaded necklace is unmistakably a marker of Indigenous culture, and it honors a woman whose indigeneity is clearly marked, unlike the Vatican's representation of Kateri in figure 4.

Figure 7 portrays Saint Kateri in an elaborate beaded necklace in a completely different style than figure 6. In figure 7, Kateri's image itself is literally beaded into a medallion shape that is the heart of the necklace; again Kateri is represented with two braids and buckskin regalia. The cross, while present, is clearly a secondary feature to the holy woman's face and braids. In both jewelry representations (figures 6 and 7), which adorn the bodies of contemporary Indigenous women, Kateri is featured as a strong feminine figure, without the reference to virginity (lilies) that usually surrounds her. Her face is the main focal point, with the cross being a secondary feature within the representation. This representation makes Kateri more relatable, and she looks like a relative or neighbor to contemporary Indigenous peoples, rather than a figure that is far away in the heavens. These are powerful representations of Indigenous femininity, as expressed by Indigenous women themselves. When I asked canonization attendees why Kateri had such great meaning to them, the usual response was "She is one of *us*." And "She is *our* saint." These jewelry representations illustrate this meaning, as Kateri's image is remade in a way that connects with and reflects contemporary Indigenous peoples and cultures. The jewelry and banners become sacred objects as they center the vision and experience of a holy woman who

Figure 6 Saint Kateri is featured in Kateri Craig's beaded necklace at the canonization festivities. Credit: Michelle M. Jacob.

Figure 7 Saint Kateri's Indigenous likeness is literally beaded onto a medallion necklace. Credit: Michelle M. Jacob.

has known spiritual powers to help heal people, to help people transform their lives, their communities, and the Catholic Church. Saint Kateri's image is transformed into a representation that has great meaning to Indigenous peoples today, as if she were a family member to the canonization attendees who honor her, as the statement "she is one of us" implies. The cross, also important within the jewelry images, is secondary. Proud Indigenous womanhood becomes the greater meaning within this indigenized Catholic representation.

One of the most powerful ways in which Kateri intervenes in Native peoples' lives is that she provides inspiration for indigenizing the Catholic Church and its services. Statues of Kateri adorn churches and altars. Rosaries are brandished with her image. T-shirts, even iPhone covers, can become sacred objects with Kateri's image printed upon them, as shown below in a photo taken at the National Tekakwitha Conference in Fargo, North Dakota (see figure 8). Texting your friend, you can be reminded of this holy woman, who is your role model and spiritual helper.

In both images of Kateri iPhone covers, she is wearing braids and clothing that reflects her Indigenous identity. In the cover on the left, she has

Figure 8 Saint Kateri Tekakwitha iPhone covers at the 2014 National Tekakwitha Conference in Fargo, North Dakota. Credit: Michelle M. Jacob.

a buckskin dress with fringe. She wears a headband and feathers in her hair. She is surrounded by nature, with the leaves and trees behind her and the lilies in her embrace. She has a rosary around her hands. In the cover on the right she wears a belt, presumably beaded. She carries the cross and is wrapped in a blue shawl, similar to the accounts that the French Jesuits provided (a shawl to cover her smallpox-damaged eyes, to protect them from the blinding sunlight). The blue shawl also conjures up a likeness to Mary, the mother of God. On the right, she has a halo signaling her holiness within the Catholic tradition. This is in contrast to the glowing light on the left that surrounds her head, also signaling holiness, but more in tune with the nature-centered theme of the art on the left.

Both images show Kateri's face as the key focal point. She has a strong subjectivity, facing the viewer directly and with face up and eyes trained on whoever looks at her. She has a gentle expression, free of strong emotion. She seems to be ready to listen, and will certainly be listening in on your cell phone call. It is almost as if having this saintly Native woman wrapped around your iPhone is meant to encourage you to also be saintly. I gazed at the lovely images at the vendor booth, and thought to myself that these Kateri iPhone covers encourage cell phone users to "Watch what you say. Be mindful of how you conduct yourself. Aspire to be like Kateri, the kind and gentle, holy and beautiful Native woman." This is a similar inspiration that artist Nellie Edwards shared with me in an interview at the Fargo conference. Nellie's artwork is featured in the opening of chapter 4, and she credits Saint Kateri with inspiring her to express her spirituality through painting. I asked Nellie if Saint Kateri intercedes for her. She replied, "Oh I believe very much so . . . every day I ask for her intercession . . . I look to her like my sister." While Nellie is non-Native, her art, especially the pieces that feature Saint Kateri, is extremely popular with Indigenous peoples, and Nellie's vendor booth at the National Tekakwitha Conference seemed to be busy nearly all of the time. Thus, Nellie is an example of an artist who creates art that helps Indigenous peoples strengthen their relationship with the Indigenous holy woman, Saint Kateri.

Kateri's story is powerful to many contemporary Indigenous peoples. She has become an important transnational figure and has had a broad impact across hundreds of Indigenous nations. I first learned about Kateri's canonization from my Mohawk colleague, Gayle, who forwarded a news story that she had received from the Kateri devotees at Akwesasne (Wojtanik 2011). I opened the e-mail message and found that my Mohawk friend had sent a news story that was, in fact, from Yakima, Washington. The story described Kateri Tekakwitha's canonization, which was being announced, based on the verification of the miracle of a Lummi boy's healing. The bishop of Yakima had been on the committee that investigated the miracle, and Kateri's intercession was verified. A Lummi boy from the coast of Washington State was healed because of prayers that were made to a Mohawk/Algonquin woman. The news story quoted elders from the Yakama Reservation, who had been devoted to Kateri for many years. The elders rejoiced in the announcement— the Vatican finally recognizing that Kateri should be a saint. In this one news story we see how Kateri connects vastly diverse tribal peoples—from Lummi, to Yakama, to Mohawk territories. Her indigeneity, her powerful representation of a strong Indigenous feminine figure, is what speaks to so many people who seek out her spiritual power and healing.

Everyone at the canonization event was familiar with the miracle that had "clinched" Kateri's sainthood. Although several people explained that Kateri was a spiritual helper and healer in small and large ways in their everyday lives, they pointed to the healing of a Lummi boy, Jacob Finkbonner, as perhaps the most important example of Kateri's intercession to help answer the prayers of all Indigenous peoples. At the canonization festivities, Jacob, the Indigenous boy from Washington State, was honored for his special connection to Kateri. As was documented elsewhere, in 2006, Jacob was injured playing basketball. His cut became infected with necrotizing fasciitis or strep A (Thiel 2012). Doctors at the Seattle Children's Hospital expected him to die from the infection. Through family, friends, and schoolmates, a prayer chain was established to pray to Kateri Tekakwitha. Sister Kateri Mitchell, who was in the area attending to business for the upcoming National Tekakwitha Conference, was contacted. She brought to the hospital a first-class relic of Kateri Tekakwitha, a tiny sliver of her wrist bone. Together with Jake's mother, Sister Kateri Mitchell prayed to Tekakwitha to intervene on Jake's behalf and to heal him. After that day, Jake began the long process of healing. Miraculously, the boy recovered. After five years of scrutinizing the case, the Vatican agreed that indeed Kateri had intervened to save the boy's life. This was Kateri's "clinching" miracle, the final step needed to complete the sainthood process and become canonized.

For many of the canonization attendees, Kateri's canonization was a great victory. Some attendees had been involved in the social movement to advocate for Kateri's canonization for more than forty years. Other people explained that they were the second or third generations in their families to pray for Kateri's sainthood. An interesting backstory to the canonization was the long struggle that Indigenous peoples and allies had engaged in to build and sustain a movement to support Kateri becoming the first Native American saint.* While most of Kateri's followers in Rome were Indigenous peoples, there were several other people who were longtime Kateri devotees, including white clergy. Kateri had a historical connection to members of the Jesuit order, and indeed it is most common to find biographies of Kateri written by Jesuit priests, who have been writing about her devotion to Christ since the late 1600s.

While Indigenous representations of Kateri portray her as a strong Indigenous woman, the historical Catholic writings tend to promote more of a color-blind representation. For example, in the Prefatory Note of Weiser's book on Kateri, John Cardinal Wright (writing from Vatican City in 1972) proclaims:

> Kateri would be . . . the perfect "North American saint," since she was an aboriginal American and bore witness to the sanctity possible in the world that is now America before the cultural and other ethnic influences of the Old World began to assert themselves in North America. But all these are specious considerations. Just as there is profound truth in the observation . . . that the priest at the altar has no face—no ethnic features, no color, no personality born of the influence of regional strains—so it is true that the saint has no citizenship in this world that makes even minimal difference. The saint is the exemplary citizen of the universal city of God, the child of transcendent

---

*Kateri Tekakwitha is commonly referred to as the first North American saint. Pope John Paul II canonized Juan Diego, an Indigenous man who is said to have lived near present-day Mexico City from 1474 to 1578, in July 2002. However, because Diego is not connected to American Indian tribal histories, he is not embraced by Indigenous peoples of the United States in the same way as Tekakwitha.

spirit in a unique and exemplary sense. Accordingly, the emphasis of Father Weiser is on the sanctity of Kateri, not her kinship with the original inhabitants of the American soil. Moreover, as is the case with everything that Father Weiser writes or says, his motive is not to incite national or local pride, but rather that joy in the faith, which is the bond and the background of the harmony in the Communion of saints. (Weiser 1971, 9–10)

This passage demonstrates how Kateri is a border crosser. From the color-blind perspective of the Catholic Church, she crosses the borders between Mohawks, the United States, Old World, New World, and the universal city of God. Within this narrative, indigeneity is acknowledged, but quickly dismissed as making "minimal difference." Interestingly, the color-blind argument renders invisible the struggles of Red Power that were raging at the time of writing. Kateri is lifted up as a holy individual, and readers are encouraged to forget any factors that detract from the mission of the Church to bring people closer to God. In this process, Indigenous kinship is purposefully deemphasized and dismissed. This "deracialization" works to uphold a colonizing discourse that displaces the power and organization from Indigenous communities and kinship networks, and places the power into the hands of Western institutions, namely the Catholic Church. The process of shifting power and recognition out of the hands/minds of Indigenous peoples and into the hands of the Church becomes what Andrea Smith calls an ethnographic entrapment within Native studies (Smith 2014). Drawing from Denise da Silva's (2007) work on racial theorizing, Smith describes the entrapment as Native peoples being rendered "objects of discovery" who have no potential to disrupt power relations rooted in colonial logics. This disruption of Indigenous social order is a pattern that not only puts Indigenous cultures at risk, but also displaces the traditional gender norms that uphold women as equal to men (Jacob 2013, Smith 2008).

Kateri's Good Medicine, Decolonization, and Cultural Revitalization

Within Indigenous communities, the term "Good Medicine" usually refers to an experience or phenomenon that helps heal individuals and communities.

Interviewees stated that Kateri had Good Medicine, but they also referred to creating artwork that honored Kateri as Good Medicine, or simply being in the presence of other Kateri followers as Good Medicine. While this is a meaningful term within communities, scholars have yet to fully describe its meaning within the literature (Garrett and Garrett 1994). However, scholars have articulated that Indigenous healing centers on four constructs: spirituality, community, environment, and self (Portman and Garrett 2006). I view the concept of Good Medicine as contributing to these four constructs of healing. Good Medicine is thus an important part of contemporary Indigenous cultural expression, and it serves as a basis for Indigenous political negotiations that contribute to decolonization efforts. More specific to this study, Kateri's Good Medicine has the potential to heal the soul wounds of colonialism (Duran 2006, Duran and Duran 1995, Jacob 2010b, 2008, 2013). Beyond merely "talking back" to Western religion, although this, too, can be an important step toward decolonization, Kateri's powerful representation helps inspire devotees to reassert the dignity of Indigenous peoples and traditions. As I observed in my fieldwork, young adults dedicated to following Kateri are learning their Indigenous languages, picking up hand drums, sewing and wearing traditional regalia, and creating beautiful artwork and jewelry, which celebrates the first Native American saint in ways that revitalize Indigenous cultural practices. By drawing from cultural traditions in a way that affirms the importance of community, Indigenous peoples are healing themselves in a powerful way and resisting the pathologizing gaze of Western society that seeks to "fix" Indigenous peoples and communities by using Western approaches (Gone 2009, Gone 2010, Million 2013).

Mohawk women shared that Kateri "always" helps them, in matters big and small. When I asked, "Has she helped you or people you know?" the women pointed out that she had helped all of us as recently as the same morning, referring to the electricity going out in the village and threatening the plans of cooking traditional foods for the feast, which the women were hosting in honor of my visit to interview them about Kateri: "Well, she helped us this morning; the lights came back on before we came home [and cooked after church]. You know sometimes when we really need something we do a little prayer and it happens, it comes. And it doesn't hit you until

Figure 9 Kateri Circle members at a gathering at Akwesasne (with author). Credit: Gayle Skawen:nio Morse, PhD.

later." And the women at Akwesasne also shared that Kateri is indeed a protector and constant companion: "I always feel like she is watching me. I'm never scared or anything. I just pray to her and she's there."

For the Mohawk women I interviewed, Saint Kateri is a constant spiritual presence in their lives. This relationship between a saint and a devotee is not unusual. However, what makes this relationship different is that it is a spiritual kin relationship rooted in Indigenous kinship. Saint Kateri is an Indigenous Mohawk woman who is at the center of these Mohawk women's daily lives. When they honor her they not only follow a Catholic tradition of praying to a saint for intercession, but they also uphold a powerful Indigenous woman figure central to one's spiritual life. When I visited the Catholic Church in their village of Saint Regis, I was struck by the centrality of Kateri within the church. She was prominently honored in the church bulletin, on the altar, and indeed, even on the priest's vestment. The priest was wearing a vestment with a large picture of Saint Kateri sewn onto it, and he shared that the Kateri Circle women had purchased the vestment for him as a gift. The

Kateri Circle women are renowned for their generosity. When I visited them they prepared a beautiful feast of food in Kateri Circle member Judy Hemlock's home at Akwesasne. Guests from the community stopped by all day to visit and share in the food and conversation (see figure 9). I was struck by the beauty of the people and the land, including the impressive trees of the Adirondack Mountains. I write more about the need to use an Indigenous environmentalism to protect Kateri's homeland in chapter 4.

Several months after my visit to Akwesasne, during my fieldwork at the National Tekakwitha Conference in El Paso, Texas, I met the women who sewed the priest's vestment at Akwesasne, two Navajo/Diné elders and sisters, Vi and Hazel, who created their own business designing and sewing Indigenous-themed vestments. Their business, Native Blessing Way, is especially popular with Indigenous peoples buying the vestments as gifts for their clergy. Vi and Hazel explained that they had a sense of humility and pride when they witnessed their vestments being used during holy Catholic ceremonies. Their work represents an Indigenous artistic expression that places Indigenous culture and people at the center of a Catholic identity. I write more about Vi and Hazel in chapter 4, and explain how their application of Indigenous cultural teachings in their spiritual lives contributes important insights into the power of elders' wisdom in working toward healing. While *Indian Pilgrims* offers many examples of the importance of spiritual strength, building community, and reclaiming the Native feminine as sacred, one of the unifying themes held by Kateri Tekakwitha's diverse followers is that she is a figure who is responsible for Good Medicine. Kateri's followers, whether Native or non-Native, have consistently maintained this message for centuries.

Contested Meanings of Indigenous Identity and Representation

In contemporary times, non-Indigenous peoples continue to be inspired by Kateri's example and her healing power. Mary Jane Nealon, an Irish-Catholic American woman, pursued a career in the health professions in part because of Kateri's early influence in her life (Nealon 2011). In her book, *Beautiful Unbroken: One Nurse's Life,* Nealon discusses her "idolization" of Kateri, and how when she was young she read Kateri's bibliography over and over—practicing helping to minister and heal Indians suffering with smallpox. She describes her childhood inspiration in the following passage:

> When I try to remember what it was about the pull of the life of caregiver and healer, all I can recall is the hard yellow cover of the Tekakwitha book, the way she knelt over the Indians suffering from smallpox, this "Lily of the Mohawks," the sketch of her, her face disfigured from milky pocks and ulcerations. I remember the last drawing in the book, after her death, when her skin was miraculously healed. I practiced her caring gestures under my sheet, pretending it was a teepee, laying a hand on an imaginary sufferer. The sufferer with parched and cracked lips surrounded by pox lesions, who smiled up at me, the only one able to take their pain away. (Nealon 2011, 12)

Nealon's memories from childhood helped shape her interest in becoming a nurse/caregiver/healer. As a child, she played "Kateri the healer" and was captivated by the idea of being a healer with a disfigured face, who was ultimately saved from her unhealthy condition. Nealon role-played in a bedsheet teepee in her Jersey City, New Jersey home (Koven 2011). She practiced being a merciful healer to pitiful, smallpox-ridden Indians who smiled at her, the only person who could save them from their pain and heal them from their grotesque conditions.

Nealon's childhood playacting is indeed a strong American tradition, as generation after generation seeks pleasure and entertainment by "playing Indian." While role-playing as a "savage" may be fun (as in Cowboys and Indians), Nealon's version of role-playing as an idealized savage who is saved from her grotesque physical condition is perhaps an even more thrilling pursuit. Left out of this role-playing narrative are critical questions about where the smallpox came from, or how the terrible communal effects of the disease played a central role in the colonial agenda to impose a physical and cultural genocide on Indigenous peoples. Such is the trend within the American pastime of Playing Indian, as Indigenous studies scholars have noted, which ultimately serves to uphold settler colonial power structures that leave the violence of colonization unnamed and unexamined (Deloria 1998, Green 1988, Tinker 2014).

Cultural genocide of Indigenous peoples is particularly important to consider in an analysis of the complexities of Saint Kateri Tekakwitha and her symbolic meaning. In Nealon's narrative, we can see an American girl co-opting an Indigenous identity, which may seem harmless enough, but in fact cultural genocide, the erasure of Indigenous peoples and cultures, is deeply harmful and wrapped up in the histories of the Catholic Church as well as the American imagination. As Tinker states, "Cultural genocide can be defined as the effective destruction of a people by systematically or systemically (intentionally or unintentionally in order to achieve other goals) destroying, eroding, or undermining the integrity of the culture and system of values that defines a people and gives them life. First of all, it involves the destruction of those cultural structures of existence that give a people a sense of holistic and communal integrity" (Tinker 1993, 6).

Nealon's fascination with Kateri's healing powers is not the first example of a non-Indian person being overwhelmed with Kateri's influence and spiritual power. For hundreds of years, this has been the case. While Kateri lived among the French Jesuits in New France (Quebec), the priests admired her strength, determination, and focus. They wrote letters home to France to speak of this humble spiritual leader. After her death, affection and admiration grew, with priests noting that Kateri was responsible for "daily wonders" and intervention—that the people who prayed to her received God's graces every day due to Kateri's intercession.

Father Chauchetière, who knew Kateri Tekakwitha and painted the portrait that was featured at the canonization event at the Vatican, wrote letters to his Superior in France to discuss the holy power of the Mohawk maiden. In his historical biography of Kateri Tekakwitha, Daniel Sargent discusses one of the priest's letters, in which he downplays Tekakwitha's tremendous influence so he isn't accused of exaggerating the young woman's power: "We cease not to say Masses to thank God for the graces that we believe we receive every day through her intercession. Journeys are continually made to her tomb; and the savages, following her example, have become better Christians than they were. We daily see wonders worked through her intercession. Her name was Catherine Tekakwitha" (Sargent 1936, 3). The priest also gives credit to Kateri's influence on other people during prayer times, stating, "all the other Indians liked to be near her in the chapel, so that they could pray better" (Sargent 1936, 234).

Other historical accounts glorify Kateri while denigrating her Indigenous identity. For example, Edward LaMore wrote a Catholic Church–sanctioned historical romantic play about Kateri. In the work, LaMore shares that Kateri "overcame" her tribal background and identity to "blossom" into something beautiful and spiritual. He refers to her as being "like a lily in a mud pond or a daisy in a coal mine" and states she came from the "worst imaginable environment" but transcended this horrible condition to be a model of "piety and saintliness" (LaMore 1932). I analyze LaMore's work as an expression of colonial logics in chapter 4.

Why Study Indigenous Catholicism?

It is unique for a scholar interested in decolonization and Native feminism to focus on the Catholic Church. Oftentimes within critical Indigenous studies, Catholicism is written off as a site of colonization, an example of empire that has damaged our communities, cultures, traditions, and well-being. However, I think the story "on the ground" is much more complex. I think that Catholicism, like many other Western institutions, has a profound impact on our communities. I am interested in how community members are responding, reframing, and transforming Western institutions to better meet the needs of Indigenous peoples. Thus, I follow Andrea Smith's approach of going beyond a simplistic dichotomous thinking, the sort of us-versus-them mentality that can prevent new coalitions from forming. Smith discusses this theme in relation to what scholars call an "ethnographic mistake." She writes, "it is clear that when we only look at the public transcripts of Native evangelical discourse in which leaders are forced to make strategic interventions within landscapes not of their own choosing, we may miss what may be very politically radical, but can be found only in private transcripts . . . Stereotypes and assumptions can keep us—and I include myself in this category—from pursuing relationships with those who might actually share more similar political visions with us than we might have guessed" (Smith 2008, 114). Rather than "stopping" our analysis with the Cycle of Destruction illustrated earlier in this chapter, I propose that we analyze it and then create a generative pathway forward, into the Cycle of Healing, and invite all peoples to join us on this journey. On our journey toward healing, Native feminism can be a very useful tool.

Native Feminism's Contribution to Indigenous Catholicism

Native feminist scholars argue that in order to truly build sovereign nations, we need to center Native women in our analyses. "This tendency to separate the health and well-being of women from the health and well-being of our nations is critiqued in Winona LaDuke's call not to 'cheapen sovereignty' (Smith 2008, 159). Placing Native women at the center of our analyses, then, can be productive on our path toward healing. Smith states, "rather than articulating gender justice as oppositional to sovereignty, the question becomes 'What does sovereignty look like if we recenter Native women in the analysis?' (Smith 2008, 159–160).

Detailing the critical theory that Native women develop and use in their home communities, Smith concludes, "sovereignty for Native women occurs within the context of sovereignty for Native nations. It also suggests that sovereignty for Native nations cannot occur without respect for the autonomy of Native women. Work by Native grassroots organizers, such as Sacred Circle and the Boarding School Healing Project teach us the importance of collectivist thinking and strategizing" (Smith 2008, 161).

Gender justice is a crucial part of social justice. Unfortunately, there is some confusion within segments of the Catholic Church regarding the importance of gender justice. For example, feminism is not always viewed as a framework that seeks to bring about social justice, and thus complement the stakes of Catholic Social Teaching, which upholds the dignity of all humans. Rather, feminism is sometimes demonized as being "divisive" and "counter" to the larger mission of the Church. For example, Raymond Cardinal Burke made headlines in Catholic media when he spoke about feminism ruining the Church, and being responsible for a lack of men's involvement in Church ministry and the dwindling numbers of priests. Cardinal Burke, in an interview with the New Emangelization Project,* stated, "Unfortunately, the radical feminist movement strongly influenced the Church, leading the Church to constantly address women's issues at the expense of addressing critical issues important to men" (Fraga 2014).

Dichotomous thinking that pits "women's issues" against "men's issues" is divisive and prevents all peoples from coming together to collectively address shared problems, which is what a feminist agenda would propose, thus undermining the Cardinal's assumption that feminism was a "strong influence" in the Catholic Church. Rather, recentering Native women in our analysis helps nudge us out of a dichotomous (and "dead end") way of thinking that either men can have issues addressed or women can have issues addressed. If we center Native women and traditional cultural teachings, we can see that supporting the roles of women as leaders and valued counselors would be helpful for any institution, especially the Catholic Church.

However, some Catholic male leaders agree with the sentiments of Cardinal Burke's comments. Sam Guzman, founder and editor of the Catholic Gentlemen Blog, stated, "The Church was very attractive to men in the past when it was very disciplined and very organized. Men love rigorous discipline and order," and, according to the Catholic news outlet *Our Sunday Visitor*, "Guzman compared the priest celebrating Mass while facing the faithful—versus populum—to having a feminine trait of relating to one another" (Fraga 2014). Thus, seeing the priest's face during Mass is offered as evidence of the power of subversive feminist ideas, such as relating to another human.

Cardinal Burke blames the Church's feminization for the lack of men's involvement in the contemporary Catholic Church. He states, "men have also been 'really turned off' by liturgical abuses since the Second Vatican Council" because "aspects of the Church's life that emphasized the 'man-like character' of devotion and sacrifice have been shelved to the detriment of men, who . . . are drawn to 'rigor and precision and excellence'" (Fraga 2014). Other Catholic leaders have different ways of explaining the threat of feminism. For example, Doug Barry, founder of Radix, a Catholic ministry,

---

*"Emangelization" is about evangelizing men in the Catholic Church.

said, "The truth is men are hurting, men are broken and men have been discarded in many ways . . . the culture, influenced by radical feminism and other ideologies, has largely 'neutered' men and discouraged their natural instincts to be providers and defenders for their families" (Fraga 2014). Cardinal Burke blames feminism for a deficient liturgy within the contemporary Catholic Church, which he views as having lost rigor, precision, and excellence (which apparently draw men to the Church, but not women). The assumption is that women prefer an imprecise, perhaps sloppy liturgical tradition. On the other hand, Barry laments that men have lost their will to contribute to the Church, their families, and society in general; indeed, men are hurt, broken, and discarded. And we can blame feminism, Barry argues, because the power of feminism within the Church and the broader society has "neutered" men.

The argument that feminism is bad/threatening to a spiritual community is flawed. There is no need to denigrate feminism, which upholds gender justice and equality as its main principles; instead, it would be to the Catholic Church's benefit to enter more fully into the Cycle of Healing. Stronger commitments to gender justice, for example, would create a stronger collective within the Church. Rather than pitting "women's issues" against "men's issues," using a feminist lens would allow us to see how women and men share concerns, which can be addressed collectively. Traditional Indigenous cultural teachings have long held that women and men are complementary, but equal (Ackerman 2000, Jacob and Peters 2011). What makes the study of Saint Kateri so interesting, from a Native feminist perspective, is that her devotees are inspired to reclaim the Native feminine as sacred in their spiritual practices. Women are not viewed as an obstacle or threat to masculinity, but rather men can strengthen their spirituality by reclaiming the respectful relationship to the feminine as sacred. Gender justice and decolonization are restorative for everyone. Kateri is the vehicle, if you will, by which this powerful spiritual and healing work takes place. Saint Kateri offers us a helpful path forward; she can be a guide for Indian Pilgrims and their allies in a Cycle of Healing.

Spiritual healing is important not only for gender justice, but for the other main lessons of this book as well, such as addressing environmental problems, and the need for community building. When we are spiritually healthy, we care for each other, Mother Earth, and ourselves. When we are not spiritually healthy, we see a breakdown in these relationships. Spirituality is central to our ways of relating to the world and each other. It directs how we conduct ourselves. As Joy Porter articulates, "a community's spiritual framework plays an important role in informing responses to environmental change, whether that framework is simply part of the social and historical matrix of a community, or whether it directly and obviously informs decision making" (Porter 2012, xxi). We can choose what spiritual framework we use. In *Indian Pilgrims* I suggest that a decolonizing and Native feminist–informed framework will be helpful in our perpetuation of a Cycle of Healing.

Conclusion: Next Chapters in Our Journey

The following are brief summaries of the upcoming chapters in *Indian Pilgrims*. Woven throughout the chapters is the theme of spiritual responsibility: to care for the environment, to build community, and to reclaim the Native feminine as sacred. At the end of the book, readers are invited to further engage with these main lessons and to brainstorm ways to continue one's journey of activism and healing.

Chapter 2. Indigenous Environmentalism as Spiritual Responsibility: Heal Ourselves, Heal the Earth

This chapter focuses on a call to revitalize Indigenous cultural traditions and languages as a means to heal Native communities and heal Mother Earth. Strong traditions support strong people, who care for one another and the land, water, air, and all living beings. The Mass of Thanksgiving for Saint Kateri's canonization at the Vatican shows how Native culture is central to Indigenous Catholicism, with Indigenous art, song, and languages prominently honored. Indigenous cultures are tied to place; our Indigenous homelands, and Saint Kateri as the Patroness of the Environment, can inspire us to care for one another and recognize the land, water, and air as our relatives, who are gifts from the Creator. In this way, Kateri's devotees are part of an Indigenous Catholicism that Chad Hamill identified, as Catholic hymns and prayers become vehicles for spiritual power and prayer, and part of an expanding Indigenous identity of seeking the sacred (Hamill 2012).

Kateri inspires a spiritual responsibility to care for the environment, and her devotees are joining other tribal peoples in critiquing the ongoing environmental devastation of Indigenous homeland. While Indigenous peoples have long been recognized as stewards of Native homelands, no scholars have articulated a concept of "Indigenous environmentalism." In this chapter, I describe Indigenous-led movements to honor Mother Earth and draw from these examples to articulate the concept of Indigenous environmentalism, describing what it looks like in theory and practice. I examine diverse examples of activism from across Indian Country and analyze how discourses that surround Kateri Tekakwitha contribute to our understanding of Indigenous environmentalism. I begin my analysis by discussing the intertribal Water Walk presented at the National Tekakwitha Conference in Fargo, North Dakota, in which members of the Saint Kateri parish church in Minneapolis described the journey of carrying water and walking in prayer the entire length of the Mississippi River. I also examine related but distinct forms of Indigenous environmentalism taking place across Turtle Island, including the Yakama people's resistance to, and successful defeat of, a coal terminal on the banks of the Columbia River to protect a sacred fishing area; the protest of Tar Sands development and megaloads by the Nimíipuu (Nez Perce) peoples, who analyze the greed underlying resource extraction as part of an ongoing colonial assault on Indigenous peoples, connecting the resistance of Chief Joseph with the contemporary protestors who use their bodies to block the transportation of equipment used in the massive Alberta Tar Sands project; the collective wisdom of Great Lakes tribes and allies who resist the development of North America's largest open-pit iron ore mine, which is proposed upstream of reservations and adjacent to the largest freshwater lake in the world, Lake Superior; and the words of encouragement and nurturing that Alaska Native elders provide as they instruct university faculty on the purpose of education: to become a "real human being" who understands the responsibility of humans to respect and honor Mother Earth.

These diverse examples inform my conceptualization of a model of Indigenous environmentalism illustrated in chapter 2. The model is rooted in my own Indigenous cultural teachings, which honor the sacredness of our mountains. The model places Tahoma (Mt. Rainier) at the center of thinking about Indigenous environmentalism, encouraging readers to think deeply about lessons of spiritual responsibility, listening to tribal elders, Looking Downstream and Looking Upstream, and embracing allies who understand the shared responsibility of protecting Mother Earth. Native feminist theorizing helps us understand how the health and well-being of the people are tied to the health of land, water, and air. I conclude the chapter by articulating ways the Catholic community can learn from the many forms of Indigenous environmentalist activism taking place, and that Saint Kateri can serve an important role in bridging Catholic and Indigenous concerns for Mother Earth.

Chapter 3. Kateri's Guidance in Building a Spiritual Community

This chapter focuses on a call to build community. The chapter shares a story about lifting one another up by acknowledging the difficulties in community, family, and personal realms, but always striving toward healing, spiritual strength, and faith. Kateri's followers achieve this by putting one's trust into the hands of the spirit powers. Interviewees discuss how they look to Kateri as a role model and kin figure. The healing of Jacob Finkbonner, a Lummi boy, has inspired countless people, as they attribute Jacob's healing to the intercession of Kateri. As the Bureau of Catholic Indian Missions states, people have been drawn back to the Church because of Jake's story and healing (Bureau of Catholic Indian Missions 2013). Jake, then, along with Sister Clissene Lewis (an Indigenous woman whom readers will meet in chapter 3) embodies the new evangelization the Church is promoting. It is an old tradition that stretches back to Kateri Tekakwitha's life in the 1600s: Indians evangelizing themselves. Sister Clissene, in starting a new religious order that is Native-led and dedicated to ministering to Native peoples, is fulfilling a dream that Tekakwitha had several hundred years ago. In this chapter I draw from ethnographic fieldwork in Rome, at the Akwesasne Mohawk Reservation, Yakama Reservation, and the National Tekakwitha Conferences to describe how Kateri devotees focus their activism on building community. Through their community building and outreach efforts, Kateri devotees, including men and non-Native clergy, practice evangelization within Indian Country, but in ways that center and respect Indigenous cultural traditions, including fighting to protect Mother Earth and upholding the sacred relationship that Indigenous peoples have with the land. I conclude chapter 3 with a model that illustrates the principles of community building, which I see taking place among Kateri devotees. The model, illustrated on the back of a turtle, honors Kateri's membership in the Turtle Clan and encourages readers to think about the principles of Interconnecting, Honoring, Embracing Responsibility, and Instructing.

Chapter 4. The Ecstasy of Saint Kateri: Native Feminism in the Catholic Church

This chapter explores the following question: is Native and Catholic an unresolvable contradiction? Struggles for self-determined spirituality, culture, and sexuality are all connected within the ongoing disaster of colonialism. The Catholic Church is one of the most prominent and long-lasting institutions rooted in the colonization of Indigenous peoples. The Church, as a settler colonial institution, is deeply implicated in the dispossession of Indigenous peoples, and creates complexities around the symbolic meaning of Kateri Tekakwitha. This chapter critiques the settler colonial lust for controlling "virgin forests" and the narratives surrounding Kateri Tekakwitha as a "virgin Mohawk maiden." These colonial logics perpetuate a cycle of land dispossession and Indigenous disempowerment. In this process we see what Andrea Smith articulates as a raping of the land, raping of Indigenous culture, and raping of people (Smith 2005a). Osage theologian, Tink Tinker, argues that the lust for controlling Native lands and peoples is part of a deeply held colonial logic that reinforces "the abject status of the Native and the sense of intrinsic righteousness of White euro-christian domination over Indian peoples and Indian lands" (Tinker 2014, 17).

I draw from Native feminist and critical Indigenous studies literatures that articulate how boarding schools, religious persecution, and gender violence are evidence of an ongoing colonial disaster (Million 2013, Smith 2008, Costo and Costo 1987). Indigenous peoples, and women in particular, articulate the need for disaster relief and transcendence. Indigenous peoples are doing so by decolonizing history, the present, and the future. The chapter draws from interview data to demonstrate that Kateri devotees are participating in Indigenous self-determination struggles to rebuild healthy Native communities. In chapter 4, readers will learn about artists and Native elders who help us envision a path of healing. This chapter features Native Blessing Way artists Vi and Hazel, Navajo elders who place Saint Kateri at the center of their artistic expression. Readers will also meet Lydia, an elder on the Yakama Reservation who has a vision of using her ancestral homeland as a gift to build a spiritual center for her people. Central to this process is the need for Indigenous peoples to reclaim our traditions and focus on strengthening the spiritual power of our people. Saint Kateri can be our journey's guide, and she provides us with important ways to see Native feminism in an "unexpected place" (Smith 2010).

Chapter 5. Conclusion: Join the Journey of Activism and Healing

Indian Pilgrims primarily focuses on examples of Indigenous social change related to activism within the Catholic Church, and how a vision of healing can inform our efforts to care for the environment, build community, and reclaim the Native feminine as sacred. This chapter concludes the book by summarizing the lessons learned from the previous chapters, and suggesting how these lessons may bring about further healing on a broader scale. Major lessons from the book demonstrate how Saint Kateri's devotees inspire Indigenous-led movements to create a space that honors the Native feminine as spiritually powerful. The primary components of this movement-building work are as follows: drawing on traditions to build strong communities, caring for one another, strengthening the spiritual power and presence of one another, and ultimately healing oneself, one's community, and Mother Earth. In the conclusion of the book, readers are encouraged to think deeply about our economy and sources of energy. I draw from the lessons in *Indian Pilgrims* to suggest that we need a spiritual revolution in our energy system. All peoples, communities, and lands need healing. These powerful lessons can be shared to heal a greater collective society.

Saint Kateri Tekakwitha inspires countless Indigenous and non-Indigenous peoples. Her extraordinary life, accounts of her miraculous interventions, and the inspirational ways in which Native women lead the vast number of her followers are all testaments to her continued influence among contemporary peoples. As a symbol, she helps us understand the inherent contradictions of a "Native feminine spiritual power" within the Catholic Church. Next, in chapter 2, I discuss the spiritual responsibility of caring for the environment. Saint Kateri, as the Patroness of the Environment, inspires her followers to understand the importance of protecting Indigenous homelands from environmental degradation. We will examine diverse examples, including issues that urge us to develop a spiritual revolution of our energy economy. We will examine what it means to engage in Indigenous environmentalism and how doing so helps strengthen communities and provides all peoples a powerful way to strengthen their roles as caretakers of Mother Earth.

2

Indigenous Environmentalism as Spiritual Responsibility

Heal Ourselves, Heal the Earth

Ethnographic Introduction: Saint Kateri Inspires People to Care for Mother Earth

I finished browsing the beautiful jewelry at the Navajo women elders' table in the lobby of the Fargo convention center. The lobby was bustling with conference attendees who were visiting with each other and browsing and shopping at the many vendor tables, which offered Indigenous cultural items (jewelry, regalia, shawls, pottery, beadwork, artwork, such as drawings and paintings) and Catholic religious items (rosaries, keychains and statues of saints, containers for holy water, books). Near the center of the main part of the lobby was a refreshment area, where conference attendees could grab a snack between conference sessions. Granola bars, fresh fruit, water, coffee, and orange juice were available. Many elders were grateful to have a snack to keep their blood sugars stable, as diabetes is such a common ailment for our people. I grabbed a granola bar and checked my program for the room of my next session. I had been looking forward to this session, one that would focus on environmental issues. I went into the beige conference room and saw the rows of standard conference chairs, with their straight backs, and those clasps that allow the chairs to be linked together to create straight rows. I sat near the front and immediately was drawn to the artwork affixed to the podium. It was a colorful picture of a woman and water. I sat admiring the beautiful artwork, entitled "Ginibiiminaan," until the session began. The panel focused on environmental issues because, as all the National Tekakwitha Conference attendees know, Saint Kateri is the Patroness of the Environment.

Dan Langlois, who helps lead the Environmental Outdoors Program at the University of Wisconsin, Eau Claire, was one of the speakers and organizers, along with Father Mike, a priest from the Gichitwaa Saint Kateri Church in Minneapolis, and one of his parishioners, Maryanna. They discussed the Catholic basis for environmentalism, noting the recent Papal writings that urge Catholics to care for all of creation. They made the link between traditional Indigenous teachings and contemporary environmentalism. They affirmed that Catholic environmentalism can work hand in hand with traditional Indigenous practices and beliefs about caring for Mother Earth. Maryanna, who "walks the talk," spoke about one particularly exciting way that people are drawing from Indigenous cultural teachings and praying for Mother Earth. She described the Water Walks that have been organized throughout Indian Country. She spoke about water as a blessing and gift from the Creator. Maryanna told about a Water Blessing that takes place at each Sunday's Mass at Father Mike's church. This blessing ceremony is Indigenous-led and -conceived. It is a beautiful example of how Indigenous peoples are placing cultural teachings at the center of Catholic spiritual practice. The panelists connected their comments to broader social and economic issues, and they mentioned how the well-being of water is threatened by multiple contemporary dilemmas: overconsumption of material goods, agricultural chemicals, feedlot runoff, mining, and fracking. Their stories and examples made it clear that each of these dilemmas is rooted in a settler colonial framework, which privileges development, resource extraction, and the quest for capitalist profit, at the expense of Mother Earth, and the protection of Indigenous homelands and cultures.

The Water Walk is an Indigenous spiritual response to restore our people's blessed relationship with water. Maryanna spoke about how they gathered water from the Mississippi River headwaters in the north, and how a team worked together to walk the water all the way to the Gulf of Mexico, praying for the water, our people, and wellness; it was clearly a spiritual endeavor. Most *people in the audience had not heard of the Water Walk, of which, as Mary-anna shared, there has been more than one. She said that before going on her journey with the Water Walk, she asked her Catholic congregation to pray for her. She is a person who is humble and strong, caring for Mother Earth and all creation.*

Next, Dan spoke about the contemporary environmental issues of iron ore mining and sand mining for fracking. One of the world's largest iron ore mines is being proposed on Anishinaabe homeland, right next to Lake Superior. He asked, why would one think it is a good idea to put an iron ore mine next to the world's largest freshwater lake? Why would one even want to move forward with that, knowing how scarce clean water is on our planet? He spoke of how the tribes organized to resist the mine, and how many people were hesitant to support the tribes who battled the big-money interests of the mining industry. Catholic bishops were asked to make a statement; universities were asked to host forums; members of the press were asked to cover events in which tribal peoples had a voice. Overwhelmingly, he explained, there was little, if any, support for tribes; very few people even wanted to acknowledge tribal peoples' resistance. Tribal peoples are engaged in vicious battles to protect their home-lands, the health of their people, and to protect the resources that are central to their cultures. It is a time of battle in the courtrooms; in city, country, state, and federal offices; in the media; and in the everyday conversations that people have about politics, the economy, and law. Tribes are engaged in what Winona LaDuke calls "The New Indian Wars."

I noticed how audience members shook their heads in disapproval when they heard how tribal peoples' efforts to protect their homelands and cultures were being dismissed and ignored. Some sighed in frustration. Clearly this group of Kateri devotees understood Dan's point—it was as if suddenly these branches of society (Church, universities, media), which we assume would engage in discussion and debate and information sharing, all simultaneously became silent. They refused to support tribal members who were speaking about the negative consequences of mining, and by extension, refused to pro-tect Mother Earth. Dan acknowledged the public/private conundrum of our society, in which individual landowners do not want to be told what to do with their land. He also acknowledged the harsh reality of rural and poor areas, whose residents often don't feel that there is an economic choice except further development, grabbing at nearly any chance for money they have, because offers do not come their way very often. He spoke with humility, and we could tell he understood the interpersonal conflicts that are part of these complex issues.

Dan also spoke about the lesser-known environmental impact of fracking: sandstone mining. In addition to the iron ore mine that has dubious environmental impacts on freshwater sources in the Great Lakes region, sandstone is being mined to use in fracking. The areas from which sandstone is being taken are already delicate and subject to erosion, and the environmental impact of sandstone mining and fracking are detrimental to the health and well-being of both the environment and, of course, the people. The audience was stunned to hear about these problems, as we had not heard about them in the media. Some audience members began asking how we could stay connected and share information beyond the annual National Tekakwitha Conference. Some people stayed after the session and exchanged contact information, encouraging each other to keep telling the stories about how precious water, land, and air are, and how Indigenous cultural teachings can help people understand that the degradation of the environment is simply not acceptable. We left feeling concerned, but committed to pray for Mother Earth.

Caring for Mother Earth: Articulating an Indigenous Environmentalism

In this chapter, I examine the contours of an Indigenous environmentalism and ask what lessons we can learn about caring for Mother Earth. Saint Kateri Tekakwitha is the Patroness of the Environment, and her devotees, such as the presenters featured in the opening ethnographic narrative of this chapter, acknowledge the need to make a spiritual commitment to caring for Mother Earth. Yet, not all Indigenous community struggles against environmental racism are framed as acts guided or honored by Saint Kateri. In this chapter, I look broadly at diverse examples of Indigenous activism to protect Indigenous homelands. I examine how the intersections of a deep concern and commitment to spirituality and the environment are expressed in Indigenous communities across Turtle Island, and conclude the chapter by articulating how Saint Kateri can serve as an important symbol of intersecting commitments to environmentalism and spirituality, and help bridge Catholic and Indigenous communities' concerns for Mother Earth.

Although Indigenous peoples are commonly recognized as caretakers of the earth, scholars have not articulated what "Indigenous environmentalism" means. To address this gap, I discuss several examples of Indigenous peoples' struggles for caring for Mother Earth, and conclude the chapter by articulating what I describe as the four main principles of Indigenous environmentalism: 1) Spiritual Responsibility; 2) Listening to Tribal Elders; 3) Looking Downstream and Looking Upstream; 4) Embracing Allies Who Understand the Shared Responsibility of Protecting Mother Earth. Within the examples of Indigenous environmentalism that I discuss in this chapter, we will examine Indigenous teachings from Alaska, the Great Lakes, the Columbia River Plateau, and the Louisiana Bayou. A common theme across these diverse sites is that there is a powerful call for people to heal the earth and to have respectful relationships with the land. Underlying this call is the warning and recognition that humans need to better tend to the earth. I ground my critical discussion of Indigenous environmentalism in terms of the ongoing struggles in which Indigenous peoples are engaged to protect their homelands from the greed, corruption, and pollution of resource extraction by multinational energy corporations. I draw inspiration from Winona LaDuke (2014) and other articulate Indigenous struggles of the "New Indian Wars," as our tribes, communities, and allies come together to once again fight for Indigenous human rights to live, thrive, and keep our cultures intact. Caring for Mother Earth is a long-standing tradition within Indigenous cultures. Destruction of the land, water, and air means destruction of Indigenous cultures and peoples. Ultimately, it will mean destruction of all of humanity. However, we do not need to follow the path of destruction, as Indigenous cultural teachings hold within them the answers to our problems.

Tribal leaders, environmental scientists, and Catholic leaders, despite their often radically different training and approaches to understanding the natural world, share similar conclusions about the current state of Mother Earth: Humans need to return to ways that treat Mother Earth respectfully. In this chapter, I draw from multiple Indigenous communities' perspectives and discuss how this mandate, to return to caring for Mother Earth, is conceptualized from an Indigenous perspective. I analyze Indigenous examples of caring for the environment and articulate a concept that I call Indigenous environmentalism. I conclude the chapter by explaining how Indigenous environmentalism is an inclusive concept, and non-Indigenous peoples can and should serve as allies in protecting Indigenous homelands. I also comment on the ways that Saint Kateri can serve as an important bridge in bringing diverse environmental perspectives together. I begin this discussion in the north, where Alaska Native elders are urging academics to think about education in traditional Indigenous cultural terms—so that we can become "real human beings."

Listening to Indigenous Elder Teachings: Alaska Native Visions of Becoming a "Real Human Being"

Academia is often viewed as responsible for producing knowledge that will help society to address its problems. In Alaska, a group of academics realized that they were sorely unprepared to do their best work as teachers and scholars. To address their needs, they did not advocate for additional funds to further their Western training, nor did they request funds for more intense lab work or equipment. Rather, they sought to build relationships and understanding with local Indigenous peoples. They realized they had missed crucial training and intended to begin addressing their knowledge gap. In their words, "We were trying something completely new here, seizing an opportunity none of us had ever had before" (Merculieff and Roderick 2013, vii). The project, professional development for non-Native faculty at the University of Alaska Anchorage and Alaska Pacific University, was designed to "improve the learning climates at our institution [that] was designed to break some difficult silences and begin to engage in some tough but necessary conversations between the academic and Alaska Native communities in our state. We introduced Alaska Native ways of teaching and learning as both a common interest and a vehicle for exploring cross-cultural differences and commonalities . . . with hopes that we might begin to seek solutions satisfying to all" (Merculieff and Roderick 2013, iii). The project was designed to strengthen the cultural responsiveness of non-Native faculty. The faculty understood that their learning about the culture, traditions, and knowledge systems of Alaska Natives would strengthen the faculty members' abilities as scholars and teachers; they understood that an Indigenous-focused education benefits all peoples, including non-Natives.

The Alaska project resulted in a book, *Stop Talking: Indigenous Ways of Teaching and Learning and Difficult Dialogues in Higher Education*. The volume *shows* the reader what is meant by an Indigenous way of learning. For example, "This material is best experienced at an earth-based pace and understood within a context that operates largely without words." And the reader is instructed: "Stop Talking. Set down your electronic devices. Set down your books and your pens. Go outside if possible; otherwise, find a window. And then for a minute or two, let go of your thoughts and listen to the wind. Pay attention to the land you are standing on and to the living things that share your space. Breathe intentionally from the common air. Notice how you feel. Stay with it as long as possible. Return to it as often as necessary" (Merculieff and Roderick 2013, vi).

What I appreciate about *Stop Talking* is that it gently shows us what is meant by an Indigenous way of learning. To say that one values the natural world, or that there are lessons contained within the natural world, or even that one should love Mother Earth, are all good things. But what is really meant? The simple instructions given in the excerpt above remind us that we need to have a calm and consistent relationship with the natural world. We must understand the gift of the land, air, and water that the Creator provides. We are told to pay attention to all the other living things that surround us, with whom we indeed share space and breathe common air, and to remember our small part in a much larger collective. These are some of the important lessons Alaska Native peoples wanted to share with the academics who work in Alaska Native homeland.

Libby Roderick, a non-Native ally and the project leader of *Stop Talking*, takes a critical approach to understanding the history and impact of colonization within Alaska Native communities. She describes the damages done in terms of "mining," and states that her work seeks to overthrow the legacy of colonization.

For centuries, scientists, researchers, authors, businesses, corporations, military representatives, government agents, spiritual seekers, hunters, fishers, and others have come to Indian country to "mine" for data, knowledge, stories, experiences, adventure, recreation, plants, animals, natural resources, and more. Most of them have shown little concern for the local inhabitants, the suffering and dislocation caused by colonialism, and the fractured relationships left in their wake. Many have profited from or built careers on the basis of what they have taken from Native communities while failing to share the profits, attention, credit, or even results with those communities. (Merculieff and Roderick 2013, ix)

Roderick concludes with an activist call:

If we can do these two things—learn from these ancient cultures fresh ways of approaching the tasks of teaching and learning while simultaneously working to overthrow the ongoing legacy of colonization that still plagues modern Indigenous peoples—we will have accomplished a great deal. It's time—past time—to build a genuinely equitable educational (not to mention social, political, and economic) system in which Native and non-Native communities function as true partners. I am convinced that phenomenal benefits could flow for all of us—Native and non-Native, students and faculty, our institutions as a whole—if we can make this happen. (Merculieff and Roderick 2013, ix)

Spiritual Core of Indigenous Environmentalism

One of the Alaska Native elders who helped lead the Stop Talking project is traditional Aleut teacher and elder Ilarion "Larry" Merculieff. Larry describes the ways in which humans should conduct themselves:

You can recognize real human beings by how they inhabit their bodies. Real human qualities include patience, gentleness, soft-spoken, observation, consideration for people and wildlife, cooperation, non-aggression, the ability to be present in the moment, and a deep reverence and respect for all living things. In Western-dominated cultures, these qualities are often associated with the feminine and dismissed as somehow of lesser or even negative worth in the fight for survival. In the Aleut worldview, however, they are the mark of a true person and a complete human being. The way of the real human being is a proven pathway to living in long-term sustainable ways on our shared land. It can—and should—help us all deal more successfully with the daunting issues facing humankind. (Merculieff and Roderick 2013, 12)

Climate change is one of the daunting issues facing humankind. Indigenous studies scholar Victoria Bomberry writes of the urgency of addressing climate change and, in doing so, paying attention to the activism of Indigenous peoples, who have been resisting "development" that fuels climate change. She writes, "The current crisis of climate change and the push for energy development threaten the very existence of Indigenous peoples and human life on the planet. It must be clearly stated that one of the most important collective sovereign rights is the right . . . to determine not only the kind of development but whether development is even desired" (Bomberry 2012, 218). Bomberry's analysis demonstrates that Indigenous peoples have always had a critical view toward Western development projects, noting,

> Whether the resources at stake are land, water, or other natural resources, Indigenous peoples have always been vulnerable to the rapacious zest for unmitigated overdevelopment of these resources. Whether settler nations 'mined' the land agriculturally, or mined for gold and other metals, or mined for oil and water, Indigenous peoples have paid dearly. With increased globalization and new technologies for extraction Indigenous nations live in a state of constant crisis. Indigenous movements throughout the hemisphere are responding to twenty-first-century threats to the land and environment, not only in their territories but as spokespeople for the earth. (Bomberry 2012, 219)

Despite Western societies' tendency to dismiss Indigenous knowledge systems, traditional Indigenous teachings, in fact, have much to offer us as we develop everyday solutions to the complex environmental problems we are facing. Solutions must be addressed collectively, as Indigenous cultural traditions teach us (Middleton 2011). Restructuring our institutions, policies, economies, and relationships, so that each of us is called to become what Aleut culture defines as a "real human being," can provide a healing pathway forward. This approach is inclusive and calls everyone to action—as everyone has a place on the path forward. Duane Good Striker, a Blood First Nations scholar and scientist, articulates the need for a collectivist and intergenerational approach to managing natural resources: "We can always sell our land and its resources for short-term gain, but if we do, it is our children and grandchildren who will suffer" (Good Stiker 1996, 151). Approaching our problems in this manner can help address the "inertia of climate change response" that Kari Norgaard researches. As she notes, the Western response to climate change typically involves "socially organized denial," which produces a "meager response" to climate change in Western countries (Norgaard 2011).

Kateri Tekakwitha as a Real Human Being

When one examines the written accounts of Saint Kateri's life and way of being, she is repeatedly described as carrying herself in a way that Aleut peoples would deem a real human being. One might assume that Kateri would join her Indigenous relatives in the New Indian Wars to protect Indigenous homeland. She was a spiritual being who was deeply connected to the natural/spiritual worlds, and we can apply Saint Kateri's example and meaning as a symbol to understand the New Indian Wars. From an Indigenous perspective, the natural word is a spiritual world (Deloria 1992). Perhaps the most famous teaching about Indigenous views of the environment can be credited to Chief Seattle, a Lushootseed leader who lamented the settler colonial greed for Indigenous land and resources. Chief Seattle was revered as an orator, and his words captivated his audiences, including journalists. One of his speeches published in an 1887 Seattle newspaper states,

> Our religion is the traditions of our ancestors, the dreams of our old men, given them by the great Spirit, and the visions of our sachems, and is written in the hearts of our people. Your dead cease to love you and the homes of their nativity as soon as they pass the portals of the tomb. They wander far off beyond the stars, are soon forgotten, and never return. Our dead never forget

the beautiful world that gave them being. They still love its winding rivers, its great mountains and its sequestered vales, and they ever yearn in tenderest affection over the lonely hearted living and often return to visit and comfort them. (University of Washington Digital Collections)

Chief Seattle's message demonstrates an Indigenous perspective of how the spiritual world and natural world are deeply intertwined. Indigenous spirituality is tied to place; it is tied to Indigenous homeland, and we see this cultural value throughout Indian Country. Thus, an Indigenous environmentalism will be spiritual at its core. As Vine Deloria stated, "Indian religions have a sacred center at a particular place . . . and accept responsibility for it" (Deloria 2003, 66). Deloria learned an Indigenous spiritual view of land as a young boy, noting, "indelibly imprinted on my mind was the fact that the Sioux people cherished their lands and treated them as if they were people who shared a common history with humans" (Deloria 1992, 1). Deloria argues that we need to reclaim our Indigenous spiritualities, and that doing so will benefit all beings. He states, "At the deepest philosophical level our universe must have as a structure a set of relationships in which all entities participate. Within the physical world this universal structure can best be understood as a recognition of the sacredness of places" (Deloria 1992, 1–2).

Catholic perspectives also acknowledge the importance of God's creation, and the human stewardship that is needed to care for God's creation (Pope Francis 2015, Misleh 2015). Yet, given the history of conquest over Indigenous peoples and lands, there is much that Catholicism can learn from Indigenous cultures and spiritual teachings. Saint Kateri Tekakwitha provides a bridge between Catholicism and traditional Indigenous teachings, which are needed to "help us to learn once again that we are a part of nature, not a transcendent species with no responsibilities to the natural world" (Deloria 1992, 3). We are at a time where we, truly, need to heed the teachings of the people who have inhabited the land for millennia (Alfred 1995). As Deloria argues, the "lands of the planet call to humankind for redemption. . . . The planet itself calls to the other living species for relief. Religion cannot be kept within the bounds of sermons and scriptures. It is a force in and of itself and it calls for the integration of lands and peoples in harmonious unity . . . who will find people with the lands? Who will listen to the trees, the animals and birds, the voices of the places of the land?" (Deloria 1992, 292). We need to all strive to live, daily, as real human beings. "Traditional ways respect the life support systems of our planet, show us how to live sustainably, and teach us to use what we call common sense, by which we mean how to live. We need these skills more than ever today" (Merculieff and Roderick 2013, 117). This is an Indigenous elder's view of what a valued education should contain. Students must learn to respect the planet, to live sustainably. From an Indigenous perspective, the development of the whole person is crucial. Here again we see overlap with Catholic values, which are expressed in Pope Benedict XVI's Message for the World Day of Peace in 2010, when he stated:

> Can we remain indifferent before the problems associated with such realities as climate change, desertification, the deterioration and loss of productivity in vast agricultural areas, the pollution of rivers and aquifers, the loss of biodiversity, the increase of natural catastrophes and the deforestation of equatorial and tropical regions? Can we disregard the growing phenomenon of "environmental refugees," people who are forced by the degradation of their natural habitat to forsake it—and often their possessions as well—in order to face the dangers and uncertainties of forced displacement? Can we remain impassive in the face of actual and potential conflicts involving access to natural resources? All these are issues with a profound impact on the exercise of human rights, such as the right to life, food, health and development. (Pope Benedict XVI 2009)

Pope Benedict's comments urge Catholics to shake themselves out of indifference to the environmental problems we are all facing. He names several specific problems, and links them to broader issues of caring for one another, or in his words, people having rights to life, food, health, and development. At the National Tekakwitha Conference session on the environment, several Papal writings were referenced, and Kateri devotees linked these to contemporary problems across Indian Country. Conference attendees were savvy at analyzing big and small actions that were needed to restore a commitment to care for Mother Earth. At the conference, Kateri devotees discussed the need to support tribal resistance against mines, which will pollute drinking water and destroy Indigenous homeland, along with questioning our daily consumption practices, such as using disposable plates and cups.

Critiquing a Styrofoam Catholicism

If we are to care for God's creation and each other, then it is not acceptable, for example, to pray for the earth and each other, and then share a meal on Styrofoam plates with Styrofoam cups of coffee and orange juice. This issue of Styrofoam usage arose at the 2014 National Kateri Tekakwitha Conference in Fargo, North Dakota. At the workshop focused on Saint Kateri's guidance and inspiration as the Patroness of the Environment, described in the opening of this chapter, one attendee asked, "Why, at a Kateri conference, would we have Styrofoam coffee cups?" Styrofoam is a petroleum product that has dubious environmental and health implications; it is made with known toxins, and it leaches into foods and beverages (Earth Resource Foundation 2014). Common sense would tell us that we do not want to have one meal or snack using plates and cups that aren't biodegradable, which will only be used once and never fully decompose in landfills. Additionally, many conference attendees are tribal elders, who already face a host of health risks in their lives, as our people bear a disproportionate risk for cancer, diabetes, and heart disease (Liao et al. 2011, O'Connell et al. 2010). Conference attendees thought of alternatives: We can start bringing our own plates and cups from home, or rearrange our finances/donations to provide more sustainable options, possibly paper cups for all who attend. Perhaps we can take the extra time, maybe two minutes, to fill a water bottle at home or in our hotel rooms and bring it with us, so that we do not need to further deplete Mother Earth's resources. Thus, Catholic attendees were able to draw inspiration from Saint Kateri, their Patroness of the Environment. They thought of alternatives that would align their practices with their spiritual convictions. They critiqued their own Styrofoam usage, drawing from the wisdom of Indigenous cultural teachings, as well as Papal teachings.

The human responsibility to care for the natural environment is emphasized in Indigenous cultural teachings across Turtle Island. In their work
with Yup'ik peoples of southwest Alaska, Ann Fienup-Riordan and Alice
Rearden write about Yup'ik elders' instructions to recognize that humans
and the natural world are inseparable. The elders frame their teachings in
terms of personal responsibility, caring for each other and the environment,
as it is all connected:

> Given their view of personal responsibility, it is no surprise that elders make
> a connection between human impacts on the environment and the "natu-
> ral" effects of climate change. Throughout our discussions, they continually
> referred to the role of human action in the world when describing changes
> in the environment or species availability. Their insistence that "the world is
> changing following its people" logically flows from their view of the world as
> responsive to human thought and deed . . . the Western separation between
> natural and social phenomena sharply contrasts with the ideas expressed
> in our Yup'ik conversations, which eloquently focus on their connection.
> (Fienup-Riordan and Rearden 2012, 321)

We are all striving to become real human beings. It is a process, a spiritual
journey. We are capable. We have the lessons contained in traditional cultural teachings. We can collectively work to care for our environment and
ourselves, but it will take a dedication to resisting the status quo, which takes
us on the path of destruction.

Indigenous Resistance and the New Indian Wars

At the National Tekakwitha Conference, when Kateri devotees considered
the environmental disasters facing our people and Mother Earth, they discussed how Kateri Tekakwitha's life story can inspire us to draw upon the
strength of the Creator, sustaining us in difficult times. To carry out the Creator's will, as did Saint Kateri, participants reasoned, we sometimes must
say and do unpopular things, even with regard to our neighbors and family
members. We must stand up against the ecological damage of fracking and

mining that our people are now facing. Kateri Tekakwitha would not have been a very good capitalist, because of her dedication to her people's traditions. She worked hard on behalf of her people. She refused to amass wealth in the form of material things. She insisted on spiritual wealth and upheld a commitment to the greater collective's good, a lesson she learned from her Mohawk longhouse culture. In these ways, Tekakwitha can serve as a strong Indigenous model for resistance—drawing from cultural teachings to uphold the sacred covenant between Indigenous peoples and homeland. Such understandings of Tekakwitha's life place Indigenous cultural teachings at the center of Kateri's strength, character, and actions. This Indigenous Catholicism does not separate Tekakwitha from her culture. Tuscarora scholar Vera Palmer critiques Catholic writings that glorify Kateri as exceptional because of her *difference* from her tribal peoples. Parmer writes, "As the exceptional Lily of the Mohawks in these hagiographies, Tekakwitha too has been marooned—alienated and isolated, and in the name of Christ" (Palmer 2014, 292). Like Darren Bonaparte, Palmer argues for the reclaiming of Kateri Tekakwitha, who is "still an unexiled daughter of the Eastern Door of the Iroquois Confederacy" (Palmer 2014, 293). While Palmer is deeply critical of the Catholic narratives that portray Tekakwitha as saintly because she is so *different* from her Indigenous kin, Palmer explains that her critique is part of an overarching movement to decolonize the narratives about our Indigenous kin. She writes,

> The ambitious praxis of liberating a dynamic Indigenous presence and voice trapped within the sacralized canonical space of an Indian conversion narrative is an act of sovereignty and decolonization. By decolonize in this case I do not necessarily mean de-Christianize. But I do mean to render transparent the rhetorical and conceptual devices operating in the name of religious dogma that conspire to terminally alienate Natives from ontological, spiritual, and political identity with our own homelands and tribal nations. (Palmer 2014, 293)

The critique that Palmer offers is thus an example of Indigenous scholarship that reclaims and reframes narratives about Indigenous peoples. This effort is critical in the broader efforts to resist the ongoing effects of settler colonialism; it is part of the Indigenous weaponry in the New Indian Wars, and the stakes of the battles are about healing our communities and protecting Indigenous homelands. As Jeffrey Shepherd argues, resisting neocolonial politics and development is crucial in decolonization efforts (Shepherd 2010). We are constantly striving to be empowered, healthy people.

I interviewed Dorothy, a non-Native woman who lives on the Yakama Reservation, about why she attends the National Tekakwitha Conferences. Dorothy learned about Saint Kateri in 2000 and at that time Tekakwitha became very important in her life, encouraging her to get involved in American Indian ministry. She said that "it totally changed her life" and that "it put a lot of pieces together" for her. Dorothy stated that she maintains a daycare in her home on the reservation, where she was inspired to display a picture of Kateri, so that when people ask about it, she can tell them about Kateri. Dorothy mentioned that attending the Tekakwitha Conference has helped show her how she can teach about Kateri—how the holy Indigenous woman is "not like something distant, but is something in you now, around you and guiding you now. She's not something down the road and something mystic, but present in you now." I asked Dorothy if Kateri had helped her or someone she knows. She immediately thought of health issues and the need to pray for people's healing. "We have a lady in our parish and she's very sick," said Dorothy, "and I know Kateri has helped her so far. And she has just found out that she has cancer and I want to go home and give a novena. . . . I'm sure Kateri will be right there and intervene." Dorothy emphasized Kateri's relationality and relatability as strong points of connection to herself and the people she lives among, noting that Kateri "was a very normal, loving person. I think a lot of times we take a saint and think that means they are way up high and not in our midst . . . but Kateri is with us now. She is very common. She lived a life like we live."

Dorothy discussed how meaningful it was that she was able to pilgrimage to Albany, and to the nearby National Shrine that honors Saint Kateri. She was honored to walk the same grounds that Kateri did, and noted that she did not buy any souvenirs, but instead gathered a small piece of bark and some water. She felt Tekakwitha's homeland had the ability to help heal. Dorothy uses the water for blessings and to pray for the healing of her ears, as she has some hearing impairment. Dorothy views Saint Kateri as a close companion-helper, whose relation and relatability make Kateri an ideal saint upon which to rely for help. In her interview, Dorothy commented on the health problems and conflicts that she observes on the reservation and concluded, "Hang in there, Kateri, we have a long road ahead," indicating that Dorothy would continue to seek Saint Kateri's intercession when she faces, or observes, any forms of suffering in her community. Dorothy's relationship with Saint Kateri provides us with an example of how Kateri serves as an inspiration for working toward healing within one's community. Dorothy recognizes the Indigenous teaching of water being sacred, and uses water gathered from Kateri's homeland to pray for herself and for healing within the reservation community.

Native feminist scholar Dian Million asks how Indigenous communities can shift the discourse from "how to heal from dysfunction" to "how to govern ourselves so that our nations are empowered as healthy people" (Million 2013, 144–145). Million draws our attention to the long tradition of Native women who work on projects and build relationships that are generative and sustainable. Million asks, "What would it really take to sustain all life in any place for eons?" (Million 2013, 143). Indigenous spiritualties are rooted in place. Thus, protecting Indigenous homeland is part of protecting Indigenous religious freedom. "Indigenous spirituality arose from the relations in a way of life, not separately" (Million 2013, 121). Steven Newcomb (Lanape/Shawnee) writes of the urgent need to reject colonizing views toward Indigenous homeland. He reminds us of the need to remember our spiritual connectedness to the natural world: "As Indigenous nations and people, we must invite the world to walk with us on this beautiful path of life in keeping with a central teaching of Indigenous law: Respect the Earth as our Mother, and Have a Sacred Regard for all Living Things" (Newcomb 2008, 136). Yet, Western cultural views continue to attempt to discount this fundamental truth. When there is a capitalist gain to be made by trampling on the rights of Indigenous peoples or traditional spiritual ways, nation-states often rule in favor of capitalist interests. Thus, the status quo of economic development tends to be one that is framed within the logic of predatory capitalism, which negatively impacts Indigenous peoples and cultures (Gutiérrez Nájera, Castellanos, and Aldama 2012, 14).

Dispossessing Indigenous peoples of their land in order to further the colonial project is a deeply held logic that has been maintained by settler colonial nation-states. Sandra Gonzales uses a critical Indigenous studies perspective of this quest for economic development. She draws from Newcomb's analysis of religion as a tool for colonization, noting that Christian "discovery" was at the heart of the colonial logic of land dispossession and the erasure of Indigenous peoples and cultures. Gonzales notes that this colonial logic legitimized the violence of colonization in the eyes of colonial agents. "The laws that native people had lived by for thousands of years were craftily negated by colonial civil law. Since the Indian had not 'subdued' the land in accordance with civil law, it was considered available for the taking, whether native people lived on it or not" (Gonzales 2012, 316). Sister Marie Therese Archambault connects the struggles of her Lakota people historically to the contemporary disasters that greed and Western capitalism have created: "One hundred years ago, Black Elk faced many hard choices: how to express himself in a changed society; how to unify in himself diverse religious traditions; how to survive economically in a world that no longer valued his cultural gifts. We who live at the dawn of a new century, face similar decisions about how to achieve our spiritual goals in a world threatened by environmental destruction, warfare and rampant materialism" (Archambault 1998, 101). Sister Archambault looks to one of her people's great spiritual leaders, Black Elk, and connects the violence of American capitalism and war-making back to the process of colonialism that challenged Black Elk's spiritual growth, as well as our own. Yet, there is hope, as Black Elk's strong example and Sister Archambault's critical analysis remind us.

Black Elk, Sister Archambault, and many others show us there are powerful examples of Indigenous resistance to the Cycle of Destruction, as Indigenous peoples are actively resisting colonial logics and the destruction of Indigenous homeland. For example, in northern Wisconsin, powerful and wealthy mining interests proposed the Gogebic Taconite open-pit iron ore mine, which would be the largest iron ore mine in North America, and potentially the world (Sierra Club—Wisconsin John Muir Chapter 2015). However, the mine would be situated adjacent to Lake Superior, the largest freshwater lake in the world. The proposed mine site is on the precious homeland of Anishinaabe peoples. The first tribe to be downriver from the mine is the Bad River Band of Lake Superior Ojibwe. Tribal chairman Mike Wiggins has represented his people by being a strong voice of opposition to the mine, as "tribal leaders must protect the air and water and the ability to hunt, fish, and gather" (Simonson 2014). Indigenous studies scholar Justine Smith articulates the key conflict in the struggle over natural resources in the Great Lakes region: "As long as the Chippewa [Anishinaabeg] maintained the right to hunt, fish, and gather on ceded lands, the treaties could be used to challenge the many mining companies that wanted to begin mineral extraction in the area. Because such mining would destroy the environment, the Chippewa effectively would be prevented from being able to conduct their traditional activities guaranteed by treaty" (Smith 1996, 61). Smith's analysis clarifies that state/corporate interests to support mining are in direct conflict with Indigenous peoples' rights to maintain their traditional cultures.

Wisconsin's eleven tribes used consensus building and voted to boycott the state board that would oversee investment money from the Gogebic Taconite open-pit iron ore mine. By refusing to sit on the board, the tribes are making it clear that to accept one seat on the seven-member Mining Investment and Local Impact Fund Board would "be like a token Indian with this thing," according to Great Lakes Inter-Tribal Council director Mike Allen. Wisconsin tribes do not subscribe to the idea of healing through the supposed "holism of capitalism" as a new form of self-determination (Million 2013, 119). Rather, tribes understand that the healing and self-determination they need comes from a sacred relationship to Mother Earth. In short, the tribes will not take a share of the "breadcrumbs" from the mining investment money. Instead, they seek to "put a stop to this" and use sovereign rights to unveil "what kind of damage this mine can do for not only the tribal people, but the state of Wisconsin" (Simonson 2014). Environmental studies scholars agree that new principles of land management are needed in order to support the sovereign rights of tribes and to protect precious natural resources. For example, Stan Stevens emphasizes the need to establish guidelines that reverse the policies that have dispossessed Indigenous peoples. Stevens writes against the settler colonial state policies, which displace and marginalize Indigenous cultures, including "loss of shared life in homelands; loss of responsibility for the care of homelands; loss of access to and care for cultural sites and cultural resources; cultural and religious sites desecrated or untended; lack of recognition of territory and tenure; and lack of respect for customary law, customary institutions, customary livelihoods, and other cultural practices" (Stevens 2014, 38). Stevens links Indigenous land dispossession to the loss of culture, and notes that Indigenous identity and cultural survival depend upon conservation of Indigenous homeland (Stevens 1997).

Chairman Wiggins views the economic development model behind the proposed mine, and the promises of mining dollars, as lures to a destructive path, stating, "These communities [who are being courted by the mining interests] are sitting there being led down a slaughterhouse canal, and the state's just watching, sitting idly by" (Simonson 2014). Additionally, Wiggins, aware that mining interests tout the promise of new jobs from the mine, countered that "if job creation is the goal, then the region should pursue farming and food cooperatives," nudging people to look at collective and sustainable options that can address the need for jobs in a way that nurtures communities and Mother Earth (ibid.). The proposed mine was discussed during a session at the National Tekakwitha Conference in Fargo, North Dakota, in 2014. As described in the introduction to this chapter, one session speaker stated, why would you put the largest open-pit mine right next to the world's largest freshwater lake? It just doesn't make sense! And indeed, it does not. In March 2015, Chairman Wiggins and the collective of activists who protested the Gogebic Taconite open-pit iron ore mine celebrated an Indigenous environmentalism victory, as Gogebic Taconite, LLC (a Florida-based company) closed its office in northern Wisconsin and filed preapplication withdrawal paperwork with the State of Wisconsin, thus ending the mining project's forward progress (State of Wisconsin 2015). While Wisconsin's tribes and their allies can breathe a sigh of relief, Wisconsin's governor Scott Walker viewed the mine's halt as "unfortunate," and Wisconsin state senator Tom Tiffany, also a champion of the mining project, stated, "I believe this ore body is going to be mined at some point, whether by Gogebic Taconite or someone else" (Associated Press 2015). Thus, the principles of Indigenous environmentalism are as important as ever, as Indigenous peoples and their allies seek to protect Mother Earth and to envision an economic and political future that does not pit financial well-being against ecological well-being.

During the National Tekakwitha Conference, while Kateri devotees urged attendees to think about ways we could protect Mother Earth, I admired the Ginibiiminaan artwork affixed to the speaker podium. It was a beautiful poster that I saw in other places, including on the postcards that invited the public to celebrate Lake Superior Day, a special day of celebration in the Great Lakes region, held each year on the third Sunday in July. The Lake Superior Binational Forum* printed postcards to publicize the day and to encourage the public to be involved in celebrating "a special day that highlights the importance of the world's largest freshwater lake to the region's environment and economy" (Lake Superior Binantional Forum 2014). The front of the postcard had beautiful Anishinaabe artwork entitled "Ginibiiminaan" (Our Water). Wesley Ballinger, language specialist and artist for the Great Lakes Indian Fish and Wildlife Commission, created the artwork. Ballinger, from Mille Lacs, stated, "Ginibiiminaan symbolizes the sacredness of nibi (water) and our responsibility to keep it pure, and highlights the important role Anishinaabe women have as keepers of the water" (Lake Superior Binational Forum 2014). In his narrative, Ballinger connected the well-being of water to the well-being of women.

Women are the keepers of the water, and are responsible for helping to protect one of the greatest gifts that the Creator has bestowed upon Anishinaabe people. Women continue to uphold this responsibility to their communities and to Mother Earth. In 2013, a group of women came together for the Women's Nibi Conversation at the Mille Lacs Ojibwe Nation Grand Casino in Minnesota. The women gathered to uphold an ancient tradition of caring for the water. Inside a meeting room at the casino, the women asked what they could do in their families, communities, and organizations to care for Nibi (Women's Nibi Conversation Group 2013). They emphasized the importance of prayer, and that people should gather to pray at any space where water is held, including water towers and waste treatment centers.

---

*To view an image of the Ginibiiminaan poster, please see the Lake Superior Day website: http://www.superiorforum.org/outreach-2/lake-superior-day.

The women stated, it is "urgent that women keep doing their work and to teach one another to do this work as well" because of the "responsibility to carry on the work and grandmother teaching so as to carry forward the work of Anishinaabe" (Women's Nibi Conversation Group 2013, 1). Out of the gathering came a commitment to continue these important conversations within their families and communities. Women reached out to one another to support and encourage their outreach, to spread awareness, and to pray for the water. The local water supply is part of the sacred Nibi, which was prayed over during the Water Walk described in the opening of this chapter. Thus, in multiple ways, the women are continuing to uphold their sacred traditions and responsibilities to care for the water.

The women are doing the grassroots work of natural resource management that Stan Stevens proposes when he suggests that conservation efforts should be guided by Indigenous knowledge systems, including "the importance of traditional conservation values and beliefs, including spiritual beliefs, stewardship attitudes, and ethics that limit styles of resource use and levels of consumption, should be recognized and supported" (Stevens 1997, 7). The spiritual responsibility to water is one that is shared across Indigenous teachings. In the next section, I describe how Indigenous peoples of the Northwest are articulating their sacred relationship with water and organizing to defeat the power and influence of big energy by resisting the construction of coal terminals, which would destroy traditional salmon fishing areas.

"The River Runs through Our Veins"

Battling the energy wars of advanced capitalism is nothing new for Indigenous peoples. In the Pacific Northwest, the Yakama Nation has been consistently fighting to uphold traditional fishing and gathering rights in the face of ongoing attempts to "develop" energy resources that are held on our traditional homelands. Whether it be the Hanford Nuclear Reservation on our traditional wintering grounds, where 444 billion gallons of liquid radionuclide and hazardous waste has been pumped into the ground (Porter 2012, 105), or the Dalles Dam that flooded and destroyed Celilo Falls, our most plentiful salmon fishing site, our tribal leaders have worked tirelessly to protect our traditional cultural ways and to help protect Mother Earth (Barber 2005, Hunn and James Selam and Family 1990, Jacob 2008, 2010b, 2013). From our people's traditional cultural perspective, it is our responsibility to uphold our covenant with the Creator, who placed us on our homelands. Our tribe has made headlines more recently in the battle over coal terminals proposed along the Columbia River. To us, the river, Nch'i-wána, has sustained our people for countless generations, as it is the way that salmon return home to us from the ocean, offering themselves as a gift to our people so that we can survive. Our traditional fishermen continue to do the difficult and dangerous work of carrying on the thousands-of-years-old tradition of pulling the heavy, beautiful fish out of the fresh water in order to feed and nurture our people. Each year, our traditional spiritual leaders carry on the legacy of honoring salmon, Waykáanash, as one of our First Foods (Jacob 2008, 2013). In the Catholic mission church on the Yakama Reservation there is a quilt that hangs near the altar, crafted with love to celebrate the history of Saint Mary's Church. One of the quilt panels features a beautiful salmon jumping out of the river (see figure 8).

This artwork reminds us of the power and beauty of the fish and the water. They are blessings to us; the river is sacred to us. As Yakama Nation environmental manager Elizabeth Sanchey stated, "The river runs through our veins. It's who we are as a people, and it's our duty to protect it" (Indian Country Today Media Network 2014). Thus, when an Australian coal mining company proposed a coal export terminal on our traditional Columbia River fishing grounds, tribal leaders and community members vowed to fight to protect fishing sites and Mother Earth. Yakama tribal chairman JoDe Goudy stated, the "Yakama Nation will not rest until the entire regional threat posed by the coal industry to our ancestral lands and waters is eradicated. We will continue to speak out and fight on behalf of our people, and for those things, which cannot speak for themselves, that have been entrusted to us for cultivation and preservation since time immemorial" (O'Leary 2014). In the New Indian Wars, tribes must quickly respond with legal, political, and media tactics in order to have a chance at being successful when wealthy multinational energy corporations unleash their plans to undermine tribal sovereignty and erode the traditional cultural ways

Figure 10 Quilt at Saint Mary's Church on the Yakama Reservation. Credit: Michelle M. Jacob.

of tribal peoples, which have been sustained in a sacred relationship with Mother Earth for countless generations.

Sometimes the New Indian Wars bring together unlikely allies. An example is the case of the proposed Boardman coal export terminal, which seeks to export nine million tons of coal, which would travel by rail through the Columbia River Gorge on trains a mile and a half long. The Yakama Nation and the State of Oregon have shared interests in protecting Nch'i-wána (Columbia River), the important waterway that straddles the Oregon and Washington state borders. In the case of the proposed Boardman coal terminal, the State of Oregon issued a "landmark denial" because "the project would unreasonably interfere with a small but important and long-standing fishery in the State's waters at the project site" (O'Leary 2014). Thus, in August 2014, the State of Oregon went on record, siding with the Yakama Nation to uphold traditional tribal fishing rights along the Columbia River.

Tribes and states often disagree on legal issues relating to natural resources, with tribes empowered through sovereign rights they have always held, and through treaty rights that were secured through negotiations with the federal government as the U.S. nation-state was being established. States thus end up squabbling for rights that they believe should be in their purview, rather than viewing tribes as a distinct and greater sovereign. Additionally, the State of Oregon does not have a stellar reputation, historically, in Indian relations. The famed Oregon Trail meant a particularly harsh colonization entanglement as settlers and state-sanctioned violence pushed tribal peoples off their traditional homelands (Crawford O'Brien 2013). Perhaps most famous in the historical accounts is Chief Joseph, the famed Nimíipuu (Nez Perce) leader, whose band lived in the beautiful Wallowa Valley in what is now Oregon, but was forced from his homeland. He and his band were pursued violently and ruthlessly, forced into surrender, and then murdered. However, denial of the Boardman coal terminal was an example of tribal and state interests aligning, so that tribal rights were upheld and privileged over and above the interests of big energy. It was an Indigenous victory in the New Indian Wars. Yet, the wars rage on. Even after the announcement of the denial of the proposed Boardman terminal, Yakama Chairman Goudy acknowledged, "This is only the beginning of what I expect will be a long fight" (O'Leary 2014).

Resisting the Tar Sands Megaloads

Given the ongoing assaults on Indigenous peoples and homelands, perhaps it is fortunate that tribal peoples are used to long fights. The Nimíipuu (Nez Perce) peoples, whose ancestor Chief Joseph led his people in resistance with an undeniable dignity, are also engaged in battle in the New Indian Wars. The megaloads (oil extraction and exporting heavy equipment measuring as much as thirty feet wide, three stories high, and three hundred feet long), which travel to the Alberta Tar Sands, invaded Nez Perce homeland. The people responded in protest, drawing from their traditional cultural ways to resist (Johnson, Holt, and Picard 2014). As one Nimíipuu woman observed, the megaload trail eerily follows the same trail that Chief Joseph traveled in the Indian Wars of the 1800s (Johnson, Holt, and Picard 2014). Demonstrating their commitment to protecting their culture and Mother Earth, Nimíipuu peoples came together in the dark of night to block the road and insist that megaloads be banned from their sacred homeland. They drummed, sang, and prayed that their land would be protected from the alien technology, which sought to carve and destroy Mother Earth. From an Indigenous perspective, the Tar Sands extraction project represents an assault on the earth; the fracking, drilling, extraction, and massive construction of pipelines across Turtle Island, from Alberta to the Gulf Coast, is creating a wasteland. Tribal treaty rights and tribal people's ability to protect their homeland become casualties of war in the settler colonial quest to extract resources for profit in the energy wars.

When the Nimíipuu come together to pray and use their bodies to demonstrate Indigenous resistance to the energy wars, they are following in the footsteps of their ancestor, Chief Joseph, who also resisted during Indian Wars more than 130 years earlier. By holding fast to their traditional teachings, Nimíipuu are able to care for themselves and for Mother Earth (Colombi 2012). Indigenous resistance in the energy wars urges us to see the land and our relationship with Mother Earth from an Indigenous perspective. Nimíipuu are not alone in their protest, or, as the Indigenous environmental organization Honor the Earth states, "We are not protestors, we are *protectors*"(Honor the Earth 2015a). Honor the Earth supported a demonstration to call attention to the ways that resource extraction harms Mother Earth and erodes tribal treaty rights (Honor the Earth 2015b). Honor the Earth understands that the struggles of Nimiipuu to protect their homeland and cultural traditions are linked to the struggles of many Indigenous peoples. Honor the Earth demonstrates to urge the public and congressional leaders to shift energy policies, in an effort to be sustainable and environmentally responsible. The dependence on fossil fuels is not a sustainable energy policy. Honor the Earth demonstrates against the Keystone XL pipeline, which is a massive construction project proposed by a Canadian company to create a pipeline to carry crude oil from the Tar Sands in Alberta to the Gulf Coast in the southeastern United States. Indigenous activists were part of a larger collective protesting the Keystone XL pipeline, and in November 2015, President Obama responded by rejecting the proposed project. The media proclaimed that he was the first world leader to reject a development project because of its impact on climate change (Davenport 2015). The messages of Mother Earth's protectors remind us of our collective responsibility: We are urged to use advanced technology to create alternative forms of energy, which do not scar the earth and leave future generations with dirty air, dirty water, and the health problems that go along with environmental degradation. We are urged to create a better future. We are urged to heal ourselves and the land.

Praying in the Bayou

Saint Kateri devotees use the National Tekakwitha Conference as a place to think about and share Indigenous cultural teachings about caring for ourselves and the land. At the 2015 conference in Alexandria, Louisiana, Houma Indians and several other tribes organized sessions critiquing climate change, erosion, and the Western development projects that fuel these devastating realities across Louisiana. One session, led by Janie Verret Luster and her elder, Father Roch Naquin, featured a prayer for protection during hurricane season. Father Roch shared a cultural and environmental analysis of the increasing damages, which have accompanied hurricanes in recent times. The development has changed the bayou landscape, and the areas that used to be "buffer zones" to soak up the floodwaters are now gone through erosion or because they lost so much vegetation that the floodwaters are not absorbed. These changes mean that bayou residents are increasingly at risk for floods, and are increasingly unable to carry out costly changes to housing construction, which would protect their homes from floodwaters, nor are their homes eligible for flood insurance. This is an example of Western development continuing to dispossess Indigenous peoples of homeland, and systematically threatening the well-being of the people and their beautiful culture.

Conference attendees learned about Indigenous fishing culture in the workshop entitled "Native Spirituality Through the Beauty of the Fish 'On the Bayou' the Alligator Garfish," led by Janie and Father Roch. As a tribal elder, Father Roch shared the changes in land/water that he has seen over his life. Father Roch, Isle de Jean Charles Band of Biloxi-Chitimacha-Choctaw Indians, has witnessed a lot of cultural and social changes during his lifetime. Drawn to religious life, he overcame multiple forms of discrimination and racism, which served as barriers on his journey to the priesthood. In 1962, he became the first Native American to be ordained as a Catholic priest in Louisiana (Marcel 2015).

The bayou people and cultures are strong examples of resilience. At the session, Janie gifted all attendees with an alligator garfish scale. She and her family make beautiful artwork out of the scales, which is a way that they honor the alligator garfish. Another session at the Alexandria conference, "Living on the Bayou Embracing the Wetlands," led by Donald Dardar (Pointe-au-Chien Indian Tribe), highlighted the beautiful relationship the people have with the bayou and gulf. Shrimping traditions were featured, including the "Blessing of the Fleet" that kicks off the shrimping season. At the conference presentations, community members talked about their personal ties to development projects and big energy, with some people speaking about relatives who worked on the gulf's oil derricks. One of the biggest threats to Indigenous homeland is erosion caused by the expansion of oil pipeline infrastructure. Another related problem is the increasing salinity of water, with freshwater sources being diverted to supply larger cities and

Figure 11 Father Roch Naquin, the first American Indian priest ordained in Louisiana. Credit: Christopher J. Andersen.

their expansion. Kateri devotees look to Saint Kateri as a source of inspiration and protection regarding these troubling environmental conditions, and the theme of the Louisiana conference, chosen by the hosts, was "Saint Kateri Embraces the Wetlands." The water, land, people, and cultures persist, despite waves of environmental degradation, including one of the more recent example: the 2010 British Petroleum oil spill. The Gulf Coast region is still attempting to recover from this horrific example. Indigenous peoples continue to draw from their cultural teachings, looking to Saint Kateri for inspiration, bringing Indigenous peoples and their allies together to pray for healing: for themselves, Mother Earth, their communities, and future generations.

We are in a time of what Ojibwe scholar and activist Winona LaDuke calls the New Indian Wars. In this chapter, I have focused on examples from the Arctic, to the Great Lakes, to the Columbia River Plateau, to the Louisiana Bayou, and shared how the New Indian Warriors and their allies are fighting to protect Indigenous homeland and cultures. Like the Indian Wars of the 1800s, our people face an opposition that has much more material wealth and advanced weaponry. Across the battles I described in this chapter, we can see how distinct and geographically dispersed battles are indeed connected. The battles are connected by ways in which capitalist lust for Indigenous homelands drives an insatiable appetite to use the courts, lawmaking realms, science, and the media to attempt to crush the rebellion of the New Indian Warriors and their allies. Yet, Indigenous resistance is resilient, and non-Natives, who live near and among Indigenous peoples, increasingly understand that the health and survival of Indigenous ways means the health and survival of all peoples who live on Indigenous homeland. Dan Langlois, whom readers met in the opening of this chapter and who works to raise awareness about tribal peoples' efforts to protect Indigenous homeland from environmental degradation, is one example of this ally spirit. All peoples benefit from such efforts.

As the battles of the New Indian Wars are all linked, so too are the solutions to the battles. To conclude this chapter, I articulate the meaning of Indigenous environmentalism and propose it as a concept that can help guide the ongoing efforts to protect Indigenous homelands and cultures. Kateri Tekakwitha, as a powerful Native feminine spiritual symbol, can provide guidance in bridging Indigenous, Catholic, and environmental science perspectives about caring for Mother Earth. Like the Alaska Native elders who advised a new/old way of doing things, I argue that we need increased efforts to indigenize our institutions. The startling lack of Indigenous representation in the arenas where the battles are fought means that Indigenous perspectives are absent, when they can influence policy and practice that fuel further assaults upon Indigenous peoples and homelands. The fields of education, law, government, science, technology, engineering, and math can benefit from the influence of Indigenous teachings. We need more Indigenous representation in each of these crucial disciplines, and more people trained in ways that are respectful of Indigenous cultures and homelands. As a society, we need to "Stop Talking" and slow down to listen, understand our place in the larger collective, and sense our responsibility to Mother Earth. These are simple lessons, but they take great care and determination to implement on a daily basis within a settler colonial capitalist context. Yet, the stakes have perhaps never been higher. Too often, Western institutions tend to believe that a problem can only be solved through objective analysis. Drawing from the teachings of our beloved Indigenous elders, I call for a turn to solving problems through awareness of our spiritual responsibility (Deloria 1992).

Indigenous Environmentalism

The examples shared in this chapter present cases by which we can trace the meaning and contours of what I am calling Indigenous environmentalism, a concept inspired by the Water Walk presentation featured in the opening of this chapter. The National Tekakwitha Conferences are providing examples of a growing concern and articulation of Indigenous environmentalism, which brings together Indigenous, Catholic, and environmental science perspectives. In this chapter, I have placed the Kateri devotees' activism in conversation with other Indigenous environmentalism activism taking place across Turtle Island. The four main components of Indigenous environmentalism are 1) Spiritual Responsibility; 2) Listening to Tribal Elders; 3) Looking Downstream and Looking Upstream; and 4) Embracing Allies Who Understand the Shared Responsibility of Protecting Mother Earth. The examples in this chapter help us to understand the importance of each component of Indigenous environmentalism, and it is my hope that this discussion will inspire all peoples who are working to heal our relationship with Mother Earth. To further illustrate the importance of Indigenous environmentalism, I have developed a visual model. In the model, the four components of Indigenous environmentalism are rooted in the natural elements of my own Indigenous homeland. The powerful stories and examples of Chief Seattle and all the activists featured in chapter 2 show the importance of Indigenous environmental activism, when all four components are strongly upheld. Indigenous peoples are communicating, sharing information about their struggles to protect their homeland, and working in solidarity. Each example of Indigenous activism demonstrates a spiritual responsibility to care for Mother Earth, and the need to heed guidance from tribal elders.

The Water Walks were founded with an understanding of the need to apply the lessons of elders, who instruct us to pray for the water. By doing so, we begin to further understand our interconnectedness. The water connects those who are downstream and upstream. The women who walked the length of the Mississippi River prayed for the people and the water all along Turtle Island, as they kept the Mississippi River as their constant companion and guide. Allies are key in this struggle to protect Mother Earth, which we are all connected to, and feel the impact of Mother Earth's well-being. My Indigenous environmentalism model helps to show the connectedness of the four components of the concept. My model was inspired by the beauty of our water sources in the Pacific Northwest, and my own tribal homeland, where we rely on the sacred mountains to provide us with clean and abundant water supplies. In the model below (see figure 12), I illustrate the four principles of Indigenous environmentalism in a photo of Tahoma (Mt. Rainier). Tahoma is a mountain sacred to Northwest tribal peoples, and the mountain watches over Seattle, named after Chief Seattle, which was also the city where Jacob Finkbonner's miracle healing took place.

The Indigenous environmentalism model is an expression of the wisdom of Indigenous cultural teachings—literally place-based wisdom, as our peoples' knowledge systems are tied to our homelands. Indigenous environmentalism also is helpful for analyzing and understanding the New Indian Wars outside of Tekakwitha Conference contexts. Across Indian Country, there is a growing call for strengthening collective efforts. We each have a responsibility to learn about and protect the "wisdom of the place" where we live (Merculieff and Roderick 2013, 144). The participants of the Stop Talking project articulate the need for "institutions that respect the best of western

Clouds: Spiritual Responsibility

Glaciers: Listening to Tribal Elders

Tree line: Embracing Allies
Who Understand the Shared
Responsibility of Protecting
Mother Earth

Creekbed: Looking Downstream
and Looking Upstream

Figure 12 Four components of Indigenous environmentalism. Credit: Michelle M. Jacob and Christopher J. Andersen.

academic traditions while simultaneously honoring Indigenous worldviews and ways" (Merculieff and Roderick 2013, 165). As Libby Roderick writes,

> Indigenous orientations—including attitudes of humility and reciprocity with respect to other life forms; traditions of gift-giving; and a recognition of our profound interdependence with the complex web of life—stand in almost direct contradiction to those of the modern Western world. As a result, Native cultures are ideally positioned to offer productive critiques of mainstream Western thought and to point toward new solutions for some of humanity's pressing problems. (Merculieff and Roderick 2013, 170–171)

Osage theologian Tink Tinker provides a helpful analysis of the "pressing problems," such as those we have examined in this chapter; Tinker urges us to understand that Indigenous liberation, and the new solutions it provides, necessitates that we engage in a strong critique of capitalism (Tinker 2004).

Conclusion

We all have a spiritual responsibility to care for the environment, to recognize that the health and well-being of the people are tied to the health of land, water, and air. In helping each other and healing our relationship with the land, we are healing ourselves. When Indigenous peoples and non-Native allies work together to protect Mother Earth, they are accomplishing healing that will benefit future generations. We see powerful examples of this healing work across Turtle Island: from the hallways of universities who host Alaska Native elders in search of a new/old way of reconnecting to the spiritual purpose of education, to the beautiful Anishinaabe homeland and pristine waters of the Great Lakes region, to the banks of the Columbia River in the Pacific Northwest, to the Louisiana Bayou that continues to sustain Indigenous peoples, and to the sacred lands upon which Chief Joseph led his people. While his Nez Perce people continue to resist a colonizing vision of harmful invasion, Indigenous peoples who are holding fast to their ancestors' teachings are guiding the way to healing our lands, communities, and the planet. Tekakwitha Conference attendees have inspired the engagement of Catholic contexts as sites for Indigenous environmentalism. In this chapter, I have placed the activism of Kateri devotees in conversation with broader struggles for environmental justice across Indian Country. By caring for Mother Earth, we are carrying out our responsibility to listen to the older generations' teachings, nurturing a healthy present-day environment, and leaving a better world for future generations. In creating a better world, we are also responsible for building and nurturing healthy communities. In the next chapter, I share examples of Indigenous community building and analyze what it means to create, maintain, and nurture a healthy community.

3

Kateri's Guidance in Building a Spiritual Community

Ethnographic Introduction: Praying and Running to Nurture Our Community

*I*t is a beautiful August afternoon, with the sun high and bright in the sky. *I see rainbows in the water spray coming from the sprinklers that irrigate the pastures on our rural reservation landscape. The fields soak up the water, and the smell of damp earth permeates the air. I make the ninety-degree sharp turn onto the next paved road, attentive to the lack of shoulders or lane stripes on the rural country roads. I notice the makeshift memorials that appear here and there, often near intersections along our reservation roads. I notice the flowers, the balloons, sometimes the crosses, stuffed animals, and signs that family and friends have made and set out in loving memory of those who have died. I think about the lives lost, the bodies injured, too often, on our roads. I continue my drive west toward our sacred mountain, Patú, and am thankful that we can once again host our annual gathering. Today we will celebrate the living while remembering those who have passed on.*

I park my car in the high school parking lot, the black pavement sizzling the August heat off its surface. Our event begins with prayer and a song by our elders, then we have a community walk, in which we will silently pray for and remember all the young people we have lost to suicide and substance abuse. We walk together in a strong collective, showing our love and support for our community. As we walk in a circle, counterclockwise, we think especially about the people who have lost a child, a sibling, a best friend. We pray that our community can be spared the heartache and loss of these senseless deaths. We look to our elders, who lead us on the walk, and hope that all our youth can be blessed with long lives and that they, too, will have the opportunity to lead our people as elders. During our prayer walk, we think about the faces that represent the statistics given by the Centers for Disease Control and Prevention: American Indians have suicide rates 50 percent higher, overall death rates 50 percent higher, and deaths from motor vehicle crashes two times higher than whites (Centers for Disease Control and Prevention 2014).

The small pieces of gravel crunch under our feet as our elders lead us in our spiritual walk. After our prayer walk, we begin the lively festivities of our community event. Children run and play. Adults also test themselves in speed and endurance challenges. For the ninth year in a row, we participate in our annual Yakama Healthy Heart Track Meet. The setting for this event is the humble nonincorporated town of White Swan, on the western edge of the lower Yakima Valley on our Yakama Reservation. The cinder track on which we run our races is rutted and pocked with small holes, yet event attendees do not complain. We are happy to have the chance to celebrate the strengths of our reservation community. This event brings together a remarkably diverse set of people. Families from White Swan and other reservation towns attend and connect with relatives and neighbors. School and university employees, present and retired, offer their help as volunteers, staffing the registration table, running stopwatches at the finish-line tape, and handing out awards and T-shirts to participants. Health-care workers from the Indian Health Service clinic, including the Yakama Healthy Heart Program, the main sponsor of the track meet, volunteer and also participate as walkers and runners; they extend a smile and a word of encouragement to their clinic patients who are enjoying the sunshine and the opportunity for some cardiovascular exercise.

Community organizations, police, and tribal programs set up information and activity booths for community outreach: letting people know about exist-

ing services, offering a way for children and families to connect to the new tribal police officer recruits, and providing games and crafts for children and their families. Local farmers in this poor, rural area are also important, donating food so that no one leaves the event hungry. One of the highlights is fresh corn on the cob, picked from the field that very morning and cooked by Job Corps personnel, whose vocational education campus is nearby.

On the track, the children are running the four hundred-meter race. The six- to nine-year-old boys have determined looks on their faces as they launch themselves from the starting line. They pant exhaustedly as they cross the finish line held up by two medical clinic volunteers, who yell and cheer as the boys finish the race. Other volunteers scurry to catch the boys before they wander off to find their families, or perhaps refresh themselves with one of those delicious ears of corn. We record the finishers' names, times, and give them an award, a medal or ribbon. The results are sent to the tribal newspaper. Together, we lift up the community and celebrate healthy life-styles. Our collective presence is a reminder of the ideals on which our culture and community are built. Although health statistics may seem to doom us to a tragic existence, we resist. Our people are resilient.

Community Building and Becoming a Real Human Being

In this chapter, we will build upon the work outlined in chapter 2, which examines the richness and meaning of community building in Indigenous communities. The diverse examples highlight the ways in which different peoples enact the spirit of "becoming a real human being," which was shared in chapter 2. Throughout the chapter, I use a Native feminist perspective, keeping Native women's perspectives and contributions central in my analysis. Saint Kateri is a central figure for inspiring community building. In chapter 3, I examine the ways that Kateri Tekakwitha's guidance can teach us to build community by putting one's trust in the hands of the spirit powers. Although there are diverse interpretations of Kateri's role and meaning as a historical figure, all accounts place her as a knowledgeable member of her community. She learned the skills and crafts of a Mohawk woman through her discipline and continued practice of her skills. She participated in her Mohawk longhouse culture to learn these forms of cultural knowledge, and as Vera Palmer states, Kateri Tekakwitha can be thought of as adding rafters to the longhouse, not turning away from it (Palmer 2014). Today, over three hundred years later, Indigenous people look to Kateri as a role model, an example of a person who is knowledgeable of community customs. Being a strong community member is a trait highly valued by Indigenous peoples. As Brenda Child and Brian Klopotek write in their essay about Indigenous education, "Knowledge of a community's political system and values, of clan and kinship, of starts and seasons, of heroes and tricksters, of laws and customs—all of this knowledge was passed down orally, through participation in community life. . . . Many of these knowledge systems have been destroyed or significantly interrupted through colonial education institutions designed specifically to interrupt the intergenerational transfer of knowledge" (Child and Klopotek 2014, 3). Child and Klopotek remind us of the importance and stakes for upholding community knowledge, and that doing so is an act of Indigenous resistance.

Within this chapter, we will see how diverse Indigenous peoples draw from their cultural teachings to find answers to the problems facing our communities. Indigenous peoples are revitalizing Indigenous cultural traditions and languages, while relying on the power of prayer and the guidance of the Creator to lead our people to better futures. Indigenous traditions will heal our bodies, minds, and lands. As articulated in chapter 2, being whole, healthy people will save us and Mother Earth from the Cycle of Destruction I introduced in chapter 1. Strong Indigenous traditions equal strong people who care for one another and the land, water, and air. This message is important for Indigenous peoples, who are reclaiming and revitalizing crucial practices of community building, which are embedded within traditional cultural teachings, but it is also important for non-Indigenous peoples who live and work on Indigenous homeland, whether reservation-based or land that was taken through conquest and colonialism to establish settler colonial society. From an Indigenous perspective, all of Turtle Island is Indigenous homeland. Caring for the land is a central part of Indigenous spiritualities. Father Pat Twohy, a Jesuit priest who has lived and worked among Northwest tribal peoples for decades, and who was made an honorary tribal member in the Tulalip Tribes in 2015, has written about the ways in which Indian and Catholic spiritual paths and beliefs are intertwined, as they share several important fundamental truths, including the need to care for God's creation. Father Pat has spent his life ministering and serving Native Americans. It has been an honorable journey for him, and as he stated, "I have known generations of teachers here at Tulalip and so many great elders that I feel so much learning has been passed on to me. I hope to have many more years to walk with the people. It is such an honor and joy for me, and I would like to walk with them into the next world" (Montreuil 2015). In his writing, Father Pat encourages Native peoples to draw from their cultural teachings to strengthen their spirituality, offering example prayers or meditations that Native peoples can use along their journeys. For example, one prayer states,

> I will try to learn what I can
> To love and protect the land we live on
> And all the animals that share this land with us,
> To share whatever I have with
> My family, my friends, my neighbors.
> When someone does not live or speak honestly,
> I will try to speak out for what I hope
> Is best for everyone. I wish to keep the land
> Good for everyone. I wish to regard each person
> With respect, as much as I can (Twohy 2009, 83).

In Father Pat's prayer, entitled "What Can I Hope to Be for My People," he places Native cultural teachings at the center of spiritual practice because they have a collectivist vision. One is not only praying for oneself, but also for one's community, one's Indigenous homeland, and for all living beings with whom one shares the land. The continual return to the meaning and importance of land within the prayer is an expression of Indigenous spiritual practices, which are tied to place/land, as discussed in chapters 1 and 2.

Spiritual Guidance on Turtle Island

Saint Kateri is a member of the Turtle Clan. Indigenous peoples make the connection between her clan and the very importance of our land, our survival, on Turtle Island. According to the Saint Kateri parish in Minneapolis, which is located on Anishinaabe homeland, the turtle is sacred to many Indigenous peoples, whose oral histories recount creation stories that place North America on the back of a turtle. Water is central to all peoples' lives. The Anishinaabe people depend on clean water for their sacred food, manoomin (rice), to grow; the importance of water is abundantly clear in an Anishinaabe worldview. They pray for clean water; they pray for a healing of Mother Earth.

The Saint Kateri parish in Minneapolis also was supportive of the Women's Water Walk in 2013 (Sander-Palmer 2013). As they shared at the 2014 National Tekakwitha Conference, and as discussed in chapter 2, the Water Walk was a spiritual journey to pray for healing of Mother Earth and the people. Women prayed during the two thousand-mile journey, carrying pure water from the headwaters of the Mississippi River on Anishinaabe homeland in Minnesota to Indigenous homeland in Louisiana on the shores of the Gulf of Mexico, and praying over the land and water throughout the journey. Their Water Walk, the spiritual journey, was carrying out an ancient tradition of connecting villages and tribes through spiritual quest. The quest, in this case, was to help remind the people of the sacredness of water and the need, the urgency, to act immediately to change our ways and attitudes, clean up our water supplies, and to reaffirm our sacred relationship with water and the land.

In contemporary Catholic missionizing efforts, the dominant message has shifted to one of inclusion, with some efforts to honor and respect Native cultural traditions within Catholic celebrations. I wanted to learn more about a contemporary Catholic missionizing view of evangelism and community building. At the Tekakwitha Conference in El Paso, I asked Father Wayne Paysse, a non-Native Catholic priest serving as executive director of the Bureau of Catholic Indian Missions, what message he wanted to share about Saint Kateri. His response carries a theme of a unified family. He also calls for Indigenous-led spiritual and social-justice work. Father Paysse states,

"I think we have to continue to hope in a better world and we need to say to our younger Native American brothers and sisters that their leadership is essential in carrying on the faith and legacy of Saint Kateri. We need to bring others to the family table and share our faith and our traditions with others, Catholics and non-Catholics."

Father Paysse frames his comments in terms of "Native American brothers and sisters," a "family table" that brings diverse peoples (Catholic and non-Catholic) together, and "their leadership is essential." Ultimately, he wishes for Saint Kateri's faith and legacy to be carried on within Indigenous communities. His comments, which center around Indigenous peoples, do not mention his organization, the Bureau of Catholic Indian Missions, one of the sponsors of the National Tekakwitha Conference, which is a national nonprofit Catholic organization that is Indigenous led. The conference brings together hundreds of American Indian Catholics every July, around the time of Saint Kateri's feast day. A different Indigenous community hosts the National Tekakwitha Conference annually. When I interviewed Father Paysse at the 2013 conference, Tigua peoples in El Paso, Texas hosted us. Father Paysse was in attendance as a white ally in the Kateri movement. How do white allies become involved in the Kateri movement? Interviewees discussed their "great love for our Native American people" and usually pointed to an older white ally as being influential as a role model. For example, Father Paysse recounted the historical legacy of missionary work that influenced him, and ultimately prepared him for his current work at the Bureau of Catholic Indian Missions. In my interview with him, he stated:

> I love it [my work] very much. For twenty years I was a parish priest and I was also the director for the pontifical mission societies. I oversaw all the foreign mission work in the archdiocese in New Orleans, that's where I'm originally from, New Orleans, and I'm on loan to Washington, DC, to the bishops [to lead the Bureau of Catholic Indian Missions]. And I taught in the seminary, and was a spiritual director in the college seminary. I love the missions; little did I ever realize I would become the national director in Washington, overseeing all the American Indian missions. I also had a parish were we had descendants of Choctaw Indians. One of the priests, who happened to be the secretary of the Archbishop of New Orleans back in the 1800s, had a great

love for the Native American people. The priest asked the bishop many times if he would like to be released of his duties as secretary, to be a missionary on the north shore of Lake Pontchartrain that was just full of Indians. The bishop kept saying, "No, no, you're important to me; I need you here in the city." Long story short, the bishop finally gave in and said, "Okay, Father, you may go." And so his name was Adrien Rouquette. He worked among the Choctaw the rest of his life. And the Choctaw adopted him and gave him a name. I don't know the pronunciation; it means "Like a Choctaw." And in our college seminary, our seminary library is named after him, you know, Rouquette. So when I was a freshman in college, we had a Benedictine; the Benedictines run our seminary. . . . And we had a priest there who loved the Indians and he loved archaeology and when I was a freshman he was telling us about the Indians, so I was always intrigued with Indians, okay. When I was ordained a priest I went off and met Saint Kateri at her tomb [in] Canada and Kahnawake. Then, I of course became a pastor where we had Choctaw Indians, and descendants of Choctaw Indians, so I think the Lord throughout my life has been preparing me for my work here in Washington, DC.

Father Paysse views his work with Indian missions as God's plan. He believes that the Lord has been preparing him, placing the people and opportunities in his life that prepared him to become the person who oversees all the Indian missions in the United States. He discusses a lineage that dates back to the 1800s, with priests before him feeling called to work with, and love, Native American peoples. The historical record verifies Father Paysse's story about Adrien Rouquette, who was recognized as a gifted intellectual and writer, who was shipped back and forth from Louisiana to Paris, where he completed important writings. His talents were greatly valued by the archbishop of New Orleans, but every time he had a choice of where to live and work, he consistently abandoned working in the Church bureaucracy, because he was happiest living among the Choctaw peoples. There was ongoing concern about needing to distract Rouquette's mind from his "savage associates." One source discusses his success as a priest in New Orleans for fourteen years, and "then suddenly, in 1859, he severed all connection with civilization and made his home for twenty-nine years as a missionary among the Choctaw Indians on the banks of Bayou La Combe" (Elder

1912). Perhaps Rouquette was entering into his own Cycle of Healing in his life among Choctaw peoples. Father Paysse is following in the footsteps of these Catholic priests, whom he regards as his inspiration. Father Paysse also acknowledges that pilgrimaging to Saint Kateri's tomb in Canada had an influence on his professional, spiritual, and personal journey as a highly public missionary leader who oversees all American Indian missions, and that he feels a special bond and kinship with the people his organization serves.

The theme of family/kinship as central to the Kateri movement was present in Father Paysse's discussion of the National Tekakwitha Conferences feeling like a "family reunion." He stated, "And as people have said in the past, and it's the truth, it's [Tekakwitha Conference] like a family reunion. So it's joyful for me to come personally to be with people and to celebrate the legacy and great heritage of our Native Americans across the country and of course under the patronage of dear Saint Kateri. Now we can say *Saint Kateri*." Annually, Kateri brings together hundreds of diverse peoples who travel great distances to attend the National Tekakwitha Conference (Thiel and Vecsey 2012, Mitchell 2012). Father Paysse discusses the conference as an opportunity to "celebrate the legacy and great heritage of our Native Americans across the country." It is striking that he states "our" Native Americans. Perhaps the use of "our" is meant in the spirit of kinship—recognizing that the conference "family" has Indigenous and non-Indigenous peoples and the conference is celebrating and honoring the Indigenous people's culture and heritage. However, "our" could also refer to the Catholic Church, so that the Conference attendees belong to the Catholic family. Or, perhaps there is a nation-state assumption behind the use of "our," as "country" (meaning the United States) is also attached to Native Americans within the quotation. Likely, it is a combination of some sort of kinship/Catholic/American identity. Saint Kateri is often conflated as an "American" saint, which is interesting neocolonial logic at work. Within this logic, Indigenous peoples are colonized subjects, and thus "belong" to the colonizing power—in this case, the United States. Kateri thus becomes a national figure for American identity, an idealized "savage" who is celebrated, tamed through the Lord's intervention and her devotion to Jesus Christ. Other Catholic accounts affirm this settler colonial logic. In the Catholic children's book *My Soul Magnifies the*

Greatness of the Lord: Saint Kateri Tekakwitha, part of the God Bless America children's book series, Saint Kateri is framed as a figure who can help inspire us to preserve a "pure Christian heart," which is needed because "God is being taken out of our society, edifying food for the soul is disappearing, [and] endangering the moral fiber" (Nippert, Nippert, and Nippert 2012).

The God Bless America book series, which features Saint Kateri and the moral panic around needing to preserve pure Christian hearts, is part of a missionizing message that views contemporary times as a threat. Yet, the message does not apply to the legacy and violence of colonization, which has indeed, from an Indigenous feminist perspective, made a good deal of "edifying food for the soul" disappear. Thus, readers of the God Bless America book series miss out on the important lessons contained within the Cycles of Destruction and Healing, lessons about what colonization and decolonization mean within narratives about Saint Kateri and contemporary Indigenous Catholicism.

There is a long history of troubling questions about naming and claiming when Christianity and Catholicism enter into Indigenous communities (Bonaparte 2009, Smith 2008, 2010). However, when Indigenous peoples become empowered to assert their traditional cultural values, reclaim cultural traditions, and assume leadership roles within the Church, then new possibilities for naming and claiming arise. For example, at the 2013 National Tekakwitha Conference, Tigua men (from Ysleta del Sur Pueblo) provided the opening blessing, praying in their Indigenous language and blessing people during a smudging ceremony (see figure 11). The men also cooked a meal, one of their traditional duties, for all conference attendees as part of a cultural celebration at the old mission. The men drew from their traditions to present their work as a blessing to conference attendees and to honor Saint Kateri, an Indigenous woman they regard as holy. The Tigua people have a shrine for Saint Kateri at their ceremonial grounds, which includes Nellie Edwards's artwork. The National Tekakwitha Conference, the organization responsible for partnering with our Tigua hosts at the El Paso conference, is led by Sister Kateri Mitchell, an Akwesasne Mohawk elder and member of the Turtle Clan (just as Saint Kateri was). Sister Kateri Mitchell's organization has done important work to place Indigenous cultural traditions and

Figure 13 Tigua men offer the opening blessing at the 2013 National Tekakwitha Conference in El Paso, Texas. Credit: Michelle M. Jacob.

Indigenous languages at the center of spiritual practices at the conference. Saint Kateri is a Native feminine figure who inspires this work. As such, she can be viewed as a figure who helps us enter into a Cycle of Healing.

To be a strong community, a group of people must sense that they belong to the community, believe in the guiding values of the community, and believe the activities that bring together the people are an expression of the values that are collectively held. Each community member must also feel that his or her presence is valued and cherished. Alienation and community disintegration happen when individuals no longer feel that they are valued members of the community; in short, their presence does not matter. Of particular importance is making sure that Indigenous youth feel valued as members of their communities. I explore specific ways Indigenous communities are engaging in community building, which uplifts and honors Indigenous

Figure 14 Yakama Reservation Tekakwitha Conference attendees (Father Paysse, back row, right). Credit: Christopher J. Andersen.

youth within an intergenerational and multicultural context. In the next section, I detail the ways that people on the Yakama Reservation are building community through gatherings focused on wellness and spirituality.

Community Belonging: Collectively Honoring Indigenous Cultural Traditions

One powerful expression of community building is the hosting and attendance of gatherings that honor culture and community. For example, in 2014, an event at Saint Mary's Church in White Swan, Washington, on the Yakama Reservation brought people together, overfilling the small mission church that sits on the western edge of the remote reservation town. One of the priests helping to celebrate the Mass, Father John Shaw, asked me to write up a reflection on the celebration. Below are my thoughts, which Father Shaw shared with Kateri devotees in a Native American ministry newsletter:

Reflections on the 125th Anniversary Celebration Mass at Saint Mary's Catholic Church in White Swan, WA

It was a beautiful, sunny Sunday morning in White Swan. The church was filled to capacity and overflow seating was needed. Family and friends greeted each other before the mass began. Everyone was looking forward to the blessed celebration of this small church with the big heart and rich history. We were treated to a bilingual English and Spanish mass, honoring the cultural diversity of the parish and community. Two choirs sang joyfully and lovingly for us, one in Spanish and one in English. Bishop Tyson gave a homily that recognized the importance of Native homeland, peoples, and culture. He recounted part of the history of the Yakama Nation and our continued spiritual strength as a people.

A particularly beautiful part of the mass was when Kateri Craig introduced the youth who performed the Lord's Prayer in Indian sign language. Kateri shared that Sue Rigdon, beloved Yakama elder and educator, had taught Kateri to sign the prayer when she was young. Now Kateri is sharing the teachings with the next generation. The youth, dressed in regalia, honored us with their performance and they represented a proud and hopeful future for our people.

I thought it was particularly fitting that Saint Kateri Tekakwitha's statue watched over us from her place of honor on the altar. The mass and the joyful spirit of the celebration reminded me of the community and kindness that guides the Tekakwitha Conference, which many of us had recently attended. The Tekakwitha Conference mission states:

Through the intercession of Saint Kateri Tekakwitha we:

- Reinforce Catholic identity;
- Affirm pride in our cultures and spiritual traditions;
- Promote healing through forgiveness and reconciliation;
- Advocate for peace and justice in our Indigenous communities;
- Build stronger religious instruction that is meaningful to Indigenous Catholics;

- Nurture the relationship between Indigenous people and the Catholic Church;
- Empower Indigenous Catholics as leaders within our communities and Church.

Thank you to all the people who lovingly prepared the mass and festivities for the community to enjoy! We are wishing Saint Mary's a happy 125th anniversary and many blessings in the future!

The 125th Anniversary gathering affirmed the importance of the Catholic faith within the community and, perhaps more strongly, affirmed the cultural diversity and strengths of contemporary church attendees. Bishop Joseph Tyson, who was on the panel that investigated Jacob Finkbonner's reported miracle, gave a homily that reminded attendees about the history of Catholicism among Yakama peoples, and how Yakamas have always been strong in spiritual dedication. The history of the church was printed on a program, which was a reminder of how much of the church's history included a handful of white missionaries, men, who were ministering to the Yakama Indians contained on the reservation. Now, the reservation is much more diverse in population. Several nuns have spent their lives in service to Yakama Reservation peoples. The church body itself is more diverse, with many Hispanic/Latino peoples now making up a large portion of church community. The 125th Anniversary Mass at Saint Mary's was bilingual, in English and Spanish, to honor this diversity. Yet, Native culture was prominent, as Saint Mary's is on Yakama homeland. The church décor featured Saint Kateri Tekakwitha prominently displayed, and the Lord's Prayer was performed in sign language by a group of young American Indians who were beautifully dressed in Indigenous regalia, led by their Yakama teacher, Kateri Craig (named after Kateri Tekakwitha), who learned to sign the Lord's Prayer from Yakama elder Sue Rigdon. Sue taught Kateri and many other Yakama youth in her work as a counselor at the Wapato Middle School and as the advisor to the Wapato Indian Club, an extracurricular club based at the Wapato Middle School. One of the main activities of the Wapato Indian Club is a traveling dance troupe that performs Yakama and other tribal dances, along with sign language performances, all of which were gifted to Sue and the club by community members and elders who volunteered their time. I profile the remarkable work of the Wapato Indian Club elsewhere (Jacob 2013). By taking the time to share the teachings with the next generation of young people, Kateri Craig is modeling the intergenerational teaching and learning principles that are at the foundation of traditional cultural teachings. Now an adult, Kateri steps into the role as teacher, and gifts the children with lessons about the discipline and respect required for learning a sign language routine, which was shared with her as a youth. Because she loves her community, she shares the teachings with the next generation.

After the Mass, the community was invited to enjoy a traditional Yakama meal of elk, salmon, and the modern delicacy of fry bread. The Saint Mary's community lovingly prepared the meal. Everyone could relish in the blessings of our sacred foods, which have sustained us for thousands of years. We could think back to the first meal enjoyed at Saint Mary's 125 years ago, with the same salmon and elk spirits offering themselves to nurture the people. Cultural performances and dances followed the meal, and the festival that brought everyone together happily celebrated the many strengths of this resilient reservation community. Featuring traditional foods was a beautiful example of how traditional foods, as a gift from the Creator, continue to be blessings that link our culture and spirituality with the natural world. Bringing traditional foods into the center of community gatherings is a healthy way to revitalize our culture and people. It reminds us what is sacred. From a Catholic perspective, the communion wafers at the church, purchased from an outside vendor and shipped to the mission church, are blessed and become holy, but for Yakama peoples, the elk and salmon are also holy—foods, gifts, from the Creator given to us and sustaining us as people since "time immemorial," as our tribal leaders say.

Keeping traditional foods alive in our communal celebrations is important in terms of keeping our community healthy. Nuu-chah-nulth scholar Charlotte Coté discusses this important point when she links cultural revitalization to the healing of Indigenous peoples. She argues, "Our leaders saw that many of the social problems that plagued our communities could be overcome by strengthening our cultures. They recognized that traditions, customs, and languages were important elements of our cultures that needed to be rejuvenated and reinforced for community growth and development"

(Coté 2010, 8). Coté discusses the importance of traditional foods in sustaining a healthy Indigenous culture and psychology. "For Native people, traditional food is sacred and has a spiritual connection to the world we live in. . . . Land, language, and food are one in an interconnected web of life" (Coté 2010, 198). Coté's work, along with the powerful example from Yakama, help inform my theorization of community building. We see how physical health and spiritual health are connected, through traditional foods, and through an understanding of connectedness to the gifts of the Creator. From a traditional Yakama cultural perspective, our traditional foods are the gifts from the Creator, which sustain us and our health. The food is a sacred covenant between our people and the Creator, Tamanwiłá.

During the week prior to the Saint Mary's celebration there was another community gathering in White Swan, the White Swan Summer Jam. I have been involved with helping coordinate some of the family wellness activities at Summer Jam with other organizations, including the White Swan Community Coalition, Yakama Healthy Heart Program, and the Center for Native Health and Culture at Heritage University. At this event, described in the opening ethnographic note of this chapter, community members from around the reservation and surrounding towns gathered to celebrate a night of drug- and alcohol-free community fun. The main event was the Yakama Healthy Heart Community Track Meet, which I discuss elsewhere, as part of a broader pattern of reclaiming health and culture on the reservation (Jacob 2010a). We hosted lap walking, running, and relay contests for all ages, with participants ranging from two years old to eighty-eight years old. All participants received a T-shirt, a ribbon, or a medal. We take seriously that every single person should have their participation affirmed. It is part of the community-building vision, which insists each person matters. We are stronger because of every person within our community.

The White Swan Summer Jam and the 125th Anniversary Celebration of Saint Mary's Church are two examples of community building, which demonstrate the power of Yakama Reservation peoples coming together to encourage and care for one another. At both events, many people donated time, money, and food to create a welcoming environment for the public. All attendees shared a meal and enjoyed visiting with old and new acquaintances. Although radically different in their structure and organization, both share the underlying premise that each individual within the community is welcomed and valued as a participant. Community gatherings like these are important points of connection—to remind us that being connected to one another strengthens our sense of community, creating good feelings and relations, which nurture us as spiritual beings who can empathize with each other. The songs sung by the choirs at Saint Mary's were gifts that lifted our spirits. The Lord's Prayer performance by Yakama youth was a gift to remind us of the importance and blessings of the next generations. The cheers and congratulations to all runners and walkers at the White Swan Summer Jam remind us all that we are strongest when each of us does our best. These examples help us to see the power and potential of community building.

Building Community through Religious Order

While the previous sections focused on examples from the Yakama Reservation, we will now examine a powerful form of community building that is taking place in the Southwest. Sister Clissene Lewis, who is Yavapai-Apache, Pima, and Hopi, tells an extraordinary story of building community that centers the needs and culture of American Indians. Sister Clissene saw that there was a need to minister to Native peoples in ways that were rooted in respect and understanding of Native cultures. To address this need, she engaged in much discernment and prayer. Ultimately, she started a new religious order, the Little Servants of the Cross. This is a profound example of a Native woman leading the efforts to engage Catholicism in ways that are fundamentally responsive to, and respectful of, Native traditions and cultures. Sister Clissene's story is documented in various newspapers and on Internet websites. The Benedictine Sisters, for example, share a story about a ceremony that Clissene's tribal community held in her honor, to mark the occasion of her journey to start a new religious order, and to draw from ancient Indigenous traditions to pray for her and her sacred journey. The story relates:

> Four Yavapi-Apache crown dancers, eagle feathers in hand, circled Sister Clissene Lewis during a Nov. 12 [2011] blessing ceremony down by the Verde

River. Three drums beat in unison through the smell of burning sage. The dancers stepped North, South, East and West, acknowledging all of creation, and through it, the Creator. A medicine man sang over the drumbeat. The blessing is a healing ceremony . . . it's prayer. The tribe blessed Sister Clissene the day she left for her novitiate year. The sister—who is a Yavapai-Apache and Pima Indian—is taking the next step in establishing a religious institute to serve Native Americans. The institute, the Little Servants of the Cross, would fill a great need in the Diocese of Phoenix, and if it grows, other parts of the country. Their name describes their mission: to be little, or humble, to serve others and to follow Jesus by accepting their cross. (Long-Garcia 2011)

The ceremony described above demonstrates how her home tribal community recognized Sister Clissene's mission to minister to her Native people. Sister Clissene's desire to build a new Catholic religious order, which was Native-led, Native-centered, and grounded in the prayerful traditions of her people, stems from her understanding of the historical trauma within Native communities. She discussed the root causes of contemporary social problems, linking the present-day social ills of violence, suffering, and substance abuse to the broader context of colonial violence and pressures to assimilate, including from the Catholic Church:

"I saw hurt, I saw the suffering of the people," she said. Sister Clissene began serving at a local Native American mission, at first just cleaning a church and helping set up for Mass. She later became a parish life coordinator at one of the missions in the Gila River Indian Community. That community struggles with rampant diabetes, gang activity and drugs. "For Native people, substance abuse comes from depression," Sister Clissene said. "That depression comes from the invasion—when our people were killed or assimilated." The conflict with European settlers is burned in Native American memory. The settlers didn't see them as human beings, she said, taking their land and putting them on a reservation. "When you destroy a people's way of life, from their language to their religion to their culture, that's demoralizing," Sister Clissene said. "That's where the infection begins." Some adults living on the reservation today attended government-run boarding schools, which forbade Natives to speak their own language and made them to cut their hair—a forced encul-turation. Children have a battle within themselves, she said, between their heritage and what mainstream culture considers success. "We're a people who are angry and frustrated," she said. "We're the poorest people in our own country." That history, and the anger that remains, presents a distinct obstacle to evangelization, she said. The Native people who are angry with "the white man" see him and his religion—Christianity—as evil. "You tell us that we can't lie, cheat, steal and then you do it in the name of your God?" she explained. "How can a Church reconcile a bad missiology? You do it through their own people, you do it through love." (Long-Garcia 2011)

Sister Clissene links the traumas facing Indigenous people today to the sys-temic violence that has attempted to destroy Indigenous languages, spiritu-ality, and culture. Her critique resonates with Vine Deloria Jr.'s analysis of the Manifest Destiny agenda, which was behind the actions of nation-states and churches that were focused on "plac[ing] the savage tribes on the evo-lutionary railroad track to civilization" (Deloria 2006, 53). Yet, despite these forced assimilation efforts, often enacted by the Catholic Church and nation-states, Indigenous people have persisted. The Yavapai-Apache blessing cer-emony for Sister Clissene is evidence of this. That Sister Clissene is leading a new religious order, specifically designed to minister to Native peoples, is significant. She is of the people and understands firsthand the need for love and prayer to heal from the multiple forms of violence inflicted upon and within Indigenous communities. This point is not lost on non-Native clergy, who comprise the majority of missionaries among Native peoples. Some officials from the Catholic Church, including within Sister Clissene's home diocese of Phoenix, anticipate that Sister Clissene can help lead a movement to encourage Native peoples to join the religious life within the Church.

Deacon Jim Trant, director of the Office of the Diaconate for the Phoenix dio-cese who's also worked in Native American ministry for years, hopes seeing "one of their own" will encourage vocations. "I'm sure nothing like this has ever happened before," he said. "Through Sister Clissene, Native American

Catholics understand they can become religious in the Church, they can become priests, they can become deacons." At first, Sister Clissene and the Little Servants of the Cross puzzled the Native community. But they've since embraced it, Deacon Trant said. The blessing from the Apache crown dancers demonstrates that embrace. "It's not a Catholic thing, this is not a Catholic community," Deacon Trant explained. "But they have great respect for it." The blessing, which Phoenix Auxiliary Bishop Eduardo A. Nevares attended, along with other priests and religious, showed a reciprocal sign of respect between the Catholic and Native traditions, he said. Sister Clissene's brother, who is not Catholic, orchestrated the blessing. "Christ died for our sins. But before the [Europeans] came here, the Creator was already speaking to us," Gordon Lewis said. "They defiled our tradition rather than learning our ways and how we serve God." Lewis said the crown dance was a sign that the Native and Catholic traditions "serve the same master." "If we felt the Catholic way was a bad way, we wouldn't do this," he said. "If we learned to be less judgmental about people's language and culture, we could be one." (Long-Garcia 2011)

Sister Clissene's story teaches us about the ways that Indigenous peoples are drawing from their sense of identity and culture to engage in community building. Since no religious order was Native-led with a specific mission to minister to Native Americans, she decided to undertake the multiyear project of starting her own religious order. Blessed by her tribe in a healing ceremony, she began her process of discernment, bringing together traditional Indigenous and Catholic traditions. This type of commitment to community building is an example of taking "the best of both worlds" discussed in the Stop Talking project, which embraced Alaska Native teachings of becoming a real human being within Western institutions. Indigenous spiritual traditions are not totalizing discourses that seek to be the "one" true way of being or praying. Clissene's new religious community seeks to build on the rich spiritual traditions of Indigenous peoples, and to do so within a Catholic context. In my interview with Sister Clissene, she discussed how elder religious people had encouraged her in her journey. For example, Sister Kateri Mitchell, the executive director of the National Tekakwitha Conference, told Sister Clissene that her mission to establish a

Native religious order was fulfilling a mission that Saint Kateri had, but was prevented from carrying out. Saint Kateri and her best friend, Marie-Thérèse, felt the power of Native women's prayer and spiritual community, and sought to establish a religious order for Native women in their praying community in New France. As a spiritually strong woman from the matrilineal Mohawk society, Kateri Tekakwitha probably would have viewed women's leadership as natural and expected. However, the young women's religious advisors, the French Jesuit priests, forbade them from organizing their own religious community, but the women continued to pray and build community in their own ways, apart from a distinct Native-led Catholic religious order. Sister Clissene draws inspiration from this historical connection between her dream and the dream young Tekakwitha had over four hundred years ago.

In her interview with me, Sister Clissene told me about her experience of first attending the National Tekakwitha Conference in 2006:

Sister Clissene: I just couldn't believe it. It was incredible and inspiring. There are all these people coming to honor this woman, Blessed Kateri, because of her courage and more than anything her fortitude in living out her baptismal call and her call from God to give him everything. And that was inspiring and to think that brought all these people together from all nations, tribes, clans in an atmosphere of love and peace and unity was truly inspiring. But again I didn't know that she desired to begin [a religious order] . . . and then I read it in a book, I think. So when I went to the conference and I met Sister Kateri [Mitchell], the Director of the National Conference, she had mentioned that [Kateri Tekakwitha wanted to start a religious order] . . . I asked her if I could share this with the attendees of the conference so they could begin praying for this new work and our community [the new religious order Sister Clissene was starting] will be called Little Servants of the Cross. So she gave me time and she also said, "Did you know that this is what Saint Kateri desired?" I told her I didn't know, but I just learned. And she said, "Yes, and I say this humbly, you could be that person; you could be the one." And I never really saw it like that, and in a way I guess it's not in the forefront of the mind or heart but I realize that is a possibility and I realize that she is with me in this journey and that it's kind of the same journey.

MJ: That you could be fulfilling the dream that Saint Kateri had.

Sister Clissene: Yes, and that our little community could stand on her shoulders.

Sister Clissene views her work in serving Native American communities as connected to a dream that Saint Kateri herself had. Kateri devotees engage in multiple forms of community building, out of a love for Indigenous communities and cultures. Strong role modeling is important in this process, including when Sister Kateri Mitchell served as a guiding elder for Sister Clissene, encouraging her to develop a religious community that would minister to Native Americans. Sister Kateri Mitchell has served as a strong advocate for bringing Indigenous cultures into the center of Catholic spiritual expression. In her writing about the need to develop culturally responsive materials that minister to Native peoples, she honors and affirms the importance of Indigenous languages and cultures, stating the "need to use our peoples' native languages. This means not only vocabulary but also cultural idioms, symbols, and thought patterns. Second, it will not be sufficient merely to adapt other catechetical materials for use in our native communities. We will need to develop new materials" (Mitchell 1996, 171). Sister Clissene shares Sister Kateri Mitchell's regard for placing Indigenous cultural traditions at the center of spiritual expression. Sister Clissene looks to Black Elk, a Lakota medicine man, as a guiding influence, which she shared in her interview with me:

MJ: You mentioned to me that Black Elk is very important to you and that he has inspired you.

Sister Clissene: Yes, Black Elk has inspired me perhaps because of his books. He lived in a very fragile time. He lived during the time reservation confinement was in the early stages, so he knew the old way of the Indian people. He was a medicine man and so he was called to God from this powerful vision as a young boy and throughout his life he was trying to make sense of that vision. I think he was 11 years old. So throughout his life he really saw that vision unfold when he entered the Catholic Church because for him the scriptures were so powerful. Particularly the gospels of Jesus, and he kind of saw himself as being a messenger. So he's able to relate to help our people as Natives, to make that connection with Catholicism, our Christian tradition.

So in a sense you could say he bridges it; the Native way of life, spiritually, and Catholicism in a profound way that I don't think many people realize, because he actually lived in that time. So he doesn't see it as a, quote unquote, *white man's religion*, but it's been termed a white man's religion because when you go into the churches you don't see anything Native if it's not on a mission church, so it kind of looks like a white church. But when I entered the Catholic Church and I stepped into my first mission church, Saint Francis, located on the Salt River Indian Reservation, it was the first time I'd ever seen a church that had Native American symbols. But the main thing it had was a tabernacle and the sanctuary light was on and I knew the Holy Eucharist, that Jesus was present through the Holy Eucharist, and when I knelt I knew I was home. So they came together as Native and Catholic and perhaps Saint Kateri might have had that same feeling.

Sister Clissene's faith journey is rooted in a strong cultural identity. She found a strong connection to Jesus when she was in a mission church that portrayed Native American culture in a positive light. This connection between Native American traditions and Catholic traditions helped Sister Clissene feel that she "was home" in the Church. She links this experiences with what she believes Kateri Tekakwitha might have felt when she began her faith journey as a Catholic. Clissene also mentions that Black Elk was a holy man who found a home in the Catholic faith. As Clissene says, Black Elk bridges the Native and Catholic spiritual lives. Sister Marie Therese Archambault agrees that Black Elk can serve as a powerful example for those who want to embrace an Indigenous Catholicism: "If Black Elk, a follower of Christ, left us an example, it is of understanding two traditions and rejecting neither. In his life, he brought unity to them in himself. Black Elk lived these two ancient traditions" (Archambault 1998, 98). Clissene has grown in her faith and leadership. She reaches out to build community and connections between Natives and Catholic traditions.

Sister Clissene finished her two-year discernment process and professed her vows in January 2014 (Benedictine Sisters of Perpetual Adoration 2014). She attended the 2014 National Tekakwitha Conference with her religious order's first Community Novice, a recent high school graduate who is currently beginning college and is discerning religious life. Perhaps she will become the next sister within the Little Servants of the Cross community. Sister Clissene mentors the young woman and helps support her in her spiritual journey. Besides mentoring the Novice, Sister Clissene is very busy traveling across Indian Country to conduct workshops and to support missionary work that ministers to Native peoples. She attends powwows and dances in her nun's habit with her beautiful shawl, which identifies her as being from Fort McDowell, Arizona. Sister Clissne proudly embraces her Native identity and her Catholic identity. She is focused on building community in ways that have Indigenous culture at its foundation. She also seeks to help transform Catholicism so that it will become a space that is welcoming and respectful of Native peoples and cultures. She upholds the idea of Indigenous principle within a Christian context (Tarango 2014).

I asked Sister Clissene what message she had about Saint Kateri for future generations. She responded,

> Every life is difficult, every life, we all have a beautiful story. It's a story of struggle and more so a story of love . . . the message would be to be like Kateri, to be open to whatever God calls you to do and act on it. So search, "God, what is your will for my life" and then follow it. An elder once said, "When you see a path, follow it to the point of knowing." How do we know something? How do we know that we are called? I asked my spiritual director that one time and he said, "We only know by doing." To seek the will of God, not my own will because our own plans can fog what God's plans are. But if we meet with God through a life of prayer as Kateri did, that's where she found her call. . . . Then say, "God, give me the heart and the courage to follow out this call, wherever you are calling me to." And do it with love and with joy. That's the message I think Kateri brings us.

Sister Clissene's desire to serve her people stems from a devotion to prayer and a commitment to healing oneself and one's community. As she mentioned earlier in this chapter, Sister Clissene understands the impact of historical trauma on Native peoples. As she stated, the need to heal is intense, as our people were "infected" by colonialism, which ravaged our people's sense of community and well-being. Sister Clissene understands that ministering to our people means working within a context that may be deeply wounded

Figure 15 Sister Clissene Lewis. Credit: Michelle M. Jacob.

with physical, mental, and spiritual illnesses. She looks to the power of spirituality, both Native and Catholic, as answers for our people's healing, and helps to articulate a theology of healing (Tinker 2014). Her Indigenous community, who blessed her on the beginning of her journey, agrees that her community building through spiritual outreach is an important mission, which benefits the entire community. Sister Clissene is a strong Native woman who is carrying out Tekakwitha's vision of a Native woman--led religious order that serves Native communities.

Men Who Honor Kateri

In the beginning of this chapter, I highlighted Father Paysse's leadership as a clergy member who honors Saint Kateri. Other men also share a devotion to the Indigenous holy woman, Kateri Tekakwitha. These men are dedicated to strengthening their own spirituality and are also community-builders in their own right. For example, I interviewed Deacon Sid Martin (Acoma Pueblo), one of the National Tekakwitha Conference staff members. He was ordained in 2000 and has been heavily involved in the Kateri movement. Deacon Sid also shared that he began to understand how important it was to pray to Kateri Tekakwitha for healing after having an industrial accident. He stated,

> We had a stage built in the memorial park . . . we were going up and down and the 4'×8' sheets [of wood] were kind of large and it was kind of awkward to balance ourselves, and I took a step back and there was no step there, so I fell backwards off the scaffold about two stories high and I landed on the back of my neck . . . and I hit the railing and I busted my arm . . . and landed on the ground, right off the concrete in the dirt, and I was kind of unconscious but I was coming out of it and everything I kept thinking was "Blessed Kateri, help me, I don't want to die. I got my wife, I got my two young kids; it's not time for me to go yet, please." So I just kept constantly praying . . . and I just felt a sense of peace and calm. And I just knew everything was going to be alright . . . they said I stayed there [at the hospital] for about three hours and they let me go.

Deacon Sid survived the terrible accident. He drew upon Western medicine as well as traditional Indigenous medicine, seeking out a bone healer among his Indigenous people in New Mexico, who helped guide him into healing and feeling better.

The accident was early on in Deacon Sid's devotion to Tekakwitha, and he stated that he felt a strong relationship with the holy Indigenous woman: "I knew from those prayers I was saying, I knew a sense of peace came over me, and I knew that everything was going to be alright." Deacon Sid has continued to serve his Native Catholic community through being involved in the Tekakwitha Conference, serving as a member of its board of directors, and by leading efforts at the local level. Sister Kateri Mitchell approached Deacon Sid to move to the National Conference headquarters (then in Montana) to help strengthen the organization, based on Deacon Sid's traditional Indigenous cultural knowledge and background. He shared that he was raised traditionally, with a strong connection to and knowledge of his Indigenous culture, including the Kiva Society, and that he later embraced Catholicism along with his traditional Indigenous teachings. Deacon Sid participates in the Healing Ceremonies at the Tekakwitha Conferences, and helps minister to conference attendees who work with him to access the spiritual world, bringing about healing in their own lives and in their relationships. Deacon Sid draws from his Indigenous community teachings to guide healing and spiritual teachings with the Tekakwitha Conference. His cultural knowledge and his love for Indigenous peoples serve as a powerful foundation for engaging in community building.

Similarly, Squi Qui/Saʔatil Ray Williams (Swinomish) also draws from Indigenous cultural teachings as a basis for his Indigenous Catholic spirituality and community building. Ray, who was serving as the executive director of the Kateri Northwest Ministry Institute, shared:

My grandmother was a very devout Catholic and, to us, she was the bridge between our spiritual ways . . . and the Church itself. She had shown us just through example you can be at [traditional Indigenous] ceremonies on Saturday night until 3 o'clock in the morning and still be the first one in church on Sunday, and she did that faithfully throughout the winters. And to me she was the example that showed me the potential for Kateri, because she's a *Native* person, Mohawk, and also Catholic; it reminded me of my grandmother, and so I became closer and closer to the movement, and to the goodness she brought unto our people, even in times of conflict in that era of history.

Ray's grandmother provided an important spiritual path, which he is continuing to follow, and Ray is extending the teachings of his grandmother by reaching out to Indigenous peoples across the Americas to better understand

Figure 16 Kateri devotee, Ray Williams, draws strength from his traditional Coast Salish ceremonies and Catholic traditions. Credit: Michelle M. Jacob.

Indigenous spiritual teachings as a pathway forward for healing and liberation. Ray views his grandmother's teachings as foundational for this spiritual work he is doing, and remembers his grandmother with love and respect:

> She found great faith in the Church and she expressed her traditional spiritual side of her as well. She was loved and respected by many . . . take a closer look at how we can blend these two worlds together. So I've been trying that for the

last 25 years and it's been very rewarding to see the parallels between the two world-views. What I believe now is that there needs to be an open dialogue . . . and I'm gearing up for that right now. I believe our ceremonial ways, and our traditional ways, are as close to God as we can get in our Indigenous life. And that the Church is a stepping stone to it . . . there can be a little tension in it, that way of looking at the world.

Ray engages in spiritual and communal work that places Indigenous self-determination at its center. In his interview, he shared that his purpose is "to see how unfairly our Indigenous people throughout the world have been treated, not only by the corporations and by the governments, but by the Church as well, and we need to balance the scales . . . I believe the Indigenous people of the world are the prophetic voice that no one hears yet, and that it's time. I think that Kateri gives us that platform to have that conversation as well." Ray works throughout the Americas and believes that this work is a path to the Creator. He credits the Swinomish/Coast Salish Winter Ceremonies back home for revitalizing his spirit, and the Tekakwitha Conferences for nourishing him, and when his work becomes challenging, he asks the ancestors and Saint Kateri to be with him. Ray has spoken at the United Nations and works broadly with activists to have discussions about the Doctrine of Discovery, Manifest Destiny, and other tragedies rooted in colonial violence. He mentioned the recent lawsuits, bankruptcies, and abuse scandals within the Church, and noted that dialogue and seeking truth will be important for moving forward in appreciation and respect for each other. When I asked Ray about how Kateri helps him combine Native and Catholic traditions, he noted that "the church is really the people." He views respect for one another and for creation as central to living as a healthy Catholic Church community. He views Kateri's sainthood as important:

> Because she is the patron saint of ecology, and she comes from the longhouse society . . . what is our true identity? It is our culture, going back to our deepest identity . . . Kateri is going to open up that door for us about the original sacred relationship with God's creation, the environment . . . we need to take a look at the ecology of the mind . . . what is imprinted into our lifeways . . . she [Kateri] represents Indigenous people of the world . . . our language is related

to the earth . . . to the creation, whether it be to the lakes, streams, rivers, oceans . . . the salmon, all the ecosystem is there, all of it has a deep relationship to us through thousands of years of interaction and through us learning through creation itself, and our language holds that.

For Ray, Indigenous culture, language, and spiritual well-being are all connected. He engages in activism to help draw attention to the need for healing and self-determination within Indigenous communities, and to have dialogues with Western institutions to seek truth in analyzing the damages of historical and contemporary forms of colonialism.

Ray's work is centered on social justice as a community-building strategy. He shares this vision with Father Mike Fitzpatrick, S.J., who is now serving as the Director of the Kateri Northwest Ministry Institute. In my interview with him, Father Mike shared that Kateri Tekakwitha has become "central" in his life, because she is the

real center of gathering for Native people and the touchstone for Native Catholic identity. And the Institute that I teach in is named for her and so she has become a real model for people, a source of hope . . . of course when the miracle occurred where Jake [Finkbonner] was healed, that her healing power that people had depended on, and prayed for, and experienced . . . it became something not just personal-devotion experience, but universally accepted by the entire faith community . . . her significance has been very major in my ministry.

Father Mike, a non-Native person who grew up in the San Francisco Bay Area, was directed to work with Indigenous peoples as part of his duties within the Jesuit order. He shared that his path started in the Omak, Washington, area in 1973, among Northwest tribal peoples. Once he arrived in Omak, to minister to Indigenous peoples there, he met a neighbor who was related to his fourth-grade teacher, who had taught him back in the Bay Area. He formed close community ties with Indigenous peoples in the Northwest, and was eventually ordained at the mission church in Omak in 1977, and he served as a priest at Saint Mary's. Eventually, he was asked to work in the Kateri Northwest Ministry Institute, where he has served Indigenous peoples from across the Northwest, traveling extensively throughout the large region. He ministers to the people by leading scripture studies, helping to prepare lectors and lay ministers, and carrying out one of the long-standing goals of the institute to teach each other. The subject matter of the institute's classes reaches beyond mainstream Catholicism; Father Mike noted that the classes are designed to be of broad interest to the people. He pointed out that one of the elders from Yakama, Yvonne Smith, had taught classes about spirituality. Other classes focused on Native identity. In our interview he also shared that classes investigate "racism and how it works and what its roots are in the colonial history of the United States, and how it still permeates all of our institutions, because it's their foundation as a matter of fact historically." Other classes focus on intergenerational trauma and unresolved grief that is rooted in colonial violence.

I asked Father Mike about how Kateri has helped him combine Native and Catholic traditions. He noted,

That's been a study that I've wanted to make. The Jesuits of course, two Jesuits, are the source for most of what we know about Kateri. So my concern also as a Jesuit, coming from the reality of the racist attitudes that underlie colonial institutions . . . including the Catholic Church, my concern has been to sort out what the lens was the French Jesuits brought . . . to try to sort out, with Native help, what was a distorting lens . . . to try as clearly as possible to understand really what was Kateri, and what was their interpretation of what was going on, and what Kateri was doing . . . and how she lived out her Native culture. So we had help last year from Darren Bonaparte, we used his book last year and went through that to try to see from Mohawk eyes . . . what was valued by Mohawk people . . . Kateri's life and example, and that was very illuminating . . . from a Native sensibility and ability to recognize, "Ah, yes, that rings true; that comes from a Native mind and heart and soul." . . . Native people participate in Catholic Christianity according to their sensibilities and life experience and culture . . . both viewing her through the history and also as a personal relationship.

Father Mike has a deep love and commitment to serving Indigenous communities. I was interested in this thoughtful and humble man's views on healing. I asked Father Mike what he thought healing would look like in Native communities. He responded,

> I guess it would be twofold. Whatever wounds continue to be experienced and suffered from the past, that are generational, carried on through generational transmission . . . that those wounds would find healing . . . the whole idea that it takes seven generations for that healing to take place, I feel I'm starting to see some signs of that healing taking place . . . and part of it is Native people have begun to be able to tell their own story. . . . Certainly with all of the boarding schools, and the sexual abuse scandals . . . hopefully with telling their own story, and having that responsibility accepted and acknowledged [by the Church], those wounds will have a chance to heal. And the other wounds of present-day racism, that is much more subtle, but ever present . . . healing from those wounds comes from a clarity of one's own identity and culture and values and vision, and that only can be given from one's own Native community . . . so that people meet the world out there "whole" and are able to speak with their own voice, and whatever prejudice, bias, blindness is there, it won't be internalized . . . the dominant society's racism . . . the generations coming up will be able to say "this is who I am, and who you think I am is not, in the end, significant to me" and that can help make a safe and fruitful place for Native people to thrive in their own way and according to their own choices.

Father Mike links his vision of healing with an antiracist message. He understands the past and present effects of the Cycle of Destruction, and views Native culture and identity as important parts of entering into a Cycle of Healing.

Because Father Mike had such a clear view of the importance of intergenerational teaching and learning, I also asked him what message he has about Kateri for future generations. He stated,

> I just hope that now that she really has been accorded the status that she has had for 300 years as a Blessed in heaven, and the Church has now recognized it, the truth of who she is and what she has to say, this is the opportune time for that to emerge. As a living person close to God, she will guide that mani-

festation that will be hopefully a path of spirit, whatever is of the spirit will become part of my identity . . . and making my way in the world . . . realizing the gifts that each one bears as part of the Native community throughout the United States and hopefully . . . all Indigenous peoples . . . that they will bring their gift to the world and that it will be something that enriches all of us. That they'll find joy.

In reflecting on some of the greatest lessons that Father Mike has learned in his work with Native people, he said,

> It's hard to put it in a few short sentences, but certainly for me it's been a rev-elation of the grandeur and the wonder and the infinite possibilities that God is. The revelation of the world and of Himself through that world to Native people really is something that can be healing for the entire world. And the Western culture that has, and the Catholic Church that has been very formed and influenced by Western history and thinking, philosophy, and technologi-cal developments that have come from it . . . the image of man that comes out of the Enlightenment . . . it is not an integral view of the human person. Native people has never suffered that history, or that philosophical leap, that abstracted them from themselves, and so for them to be who they are and share that way of life and that vision and harmony and unity of being, as an experience and a lived reality, that's been *salvific* for me, and I wouldn't change a minute of it for anything.

Father Mike's comments demonstrate the power of Indigenous cultural teachings as being central for building a sense of community that is mean-ingful and a "vision of harmony." Other white clergy feel similarly, that they have been deeply blessed to live in Indigenous communities, and that they learn about a way of being that was discussed in chapter 2 as "becoming a real human being." For example, next we will examine the experiences and thoughts of Reverend Edward Sherman, a non-Native priest who is devoted to Saint Kateri, and he wrote a book about the holy Indigenous woman (Sherman 2007). In my interview with him, he shared that he was born in 1930 and that due to his dad's work, his family had lived for the first eleven years of his life at Chemawa, Oregon, the site of an Indian boarding school.

He noted that he had some contact with the young Native students, often at social gatherings the school hosted, such as pageants and what we would now refer to as social powwows. After Chemawa, his family moved to Cherokee, North Carolina, and his family lived similarly in housing around the Indian boarding school, and then the family moved to North Dakota. In Father Sherman's first assignment as clergy at Saint John's parish, the majority of the people were Native. It was there that he learned to live in community. He said the people (Chippewa/Ojibway/Cree) taught him how to pace himself and enjoy being together with the community. He was sad to leave the community when he was transferred, but eventually he became Pastor on the Spirit Lake Reservation, and although the Dakota Sioux culture was different than the Indigenous cultures at Saint John's, he saw parallels, such as having a slower and relational pace, a comfort of being in each other's presence in community, and the tendency of not needing to talk too much during social visits. In my interview with him, he shared, "sitting down with people, and if there was a lull in the conversation, people were not nervous . . . so what? . . . and I do recall people saying . . . I'd go to the home of elders, and was always welcomed, and with greetings, 'hello,' we'd sit down, and then maybe *nothing* much was said! Except, you know, kind looks, and offer of refreshments, and things like that. And leaving, without really saying much, and then hearing later on how they'd remark to their neighbors, 'We had such a wonderful visit with Father.' And I was delighted with that!" Father Sherman's comments remind us of the Stop Talking lessons shared in chapter 2. Part of the gift of learning how to live in and contribute to Indigenous communities helped Father Sherman in his journey to become what Alaska Native elders described as "a real human being."

I asked Father Sherman when he first became devoted to Saint Kateri. Father Sherman mentioned that when he was hospitalized he read a biography of Kateri Tekakwitha, and he wondered how the author knew the things that were written, as there were no footnotes or references. Father Sherman also discussed how his sister, who was a nurse practitioner on the Pine Ridge Reservation, had a serious illness that doctors could not figure out: "If there was something wrong, she would pass out." Eventually they found out she had an insulin disorder and cancerous tumors. He told me that his sister met a priest in Rapid City, stating:

And he had a relic of Kateri and he blessed her with it . . . and I know she got some help. She did. There's no doubt about it . . . the type of cancer she had, she would have been lucky to live five years, but she lived twenty. So I'm convinced Kateri got help from our Lord. And we kept talking . . . and she took me to the library, and she knew what I was looking for. I had been writing and she kept encouraging me. She kept pulling down books. One of them was something like "Native American Who's Who" and there was an article in there, a piece on Tekakwitha. It wasn't long, maybe a page and a half, and I read it. And I asked the librarian if I could make a copy of it . . . and the author of the article was Sister Marie Therese Archambault and she was Lakota . . . and I've heard others speak of her as being very informed about Native history . . . at a conference two or three years later . . . I approached Sister, she happened to be there . . . "Would you mind taking this [draft of his book] with you? May I give you this? I would love to hear from you." I got back the most encouraging letter from her.

Father Sherman's narrative is a reflection on how living in community with Indigenous peoples has been a blessing in his life. In this section, we have examined several examples of how men are devoted to Saint Kateri, and how their devotion helps them to build community. Father Sherman represents another testimony of non-Native clergy who are part of the Tekakwitha Conference community who have had formative experiences, which have shaped their identities as allies in a spiritual movement that places Indigenous cultural teachings at the center of devotional practice. Non-Native clergy, like Father Mike and Father Sherman, state that they learn about the power and beauty of Indigenous cultures when they live in community with Indigenous peoples, and the men see how they benefit from Indigenous teachings. Father Sherman mentions Sister Marie Therese Archambault, a Lakota woman who became a Franciscan Sister and wrote a book about Lakota holy man Nicolas Black Elk (Archambault 1998). In her writings, Sister Archambault explains, "Black Elk's life reflected his conviction that this people could live again spiritually in two ways: through the Catholic tradition he embraced and through the ancient Lakota traditions. . . . He lived his last forty-six years as a staunch Catholic and firm teacher of its faith among the Oglala and several Upper Plains tribes" (Archambault 1998, 7–8). Black

Elk's cause for canonization is currently the focus of Indigenous activism, with many peoples praying for his canonization into Catholic sainthood. In his interview, Father Sherman discusses the healing power of Kateri Tekakwitha's relic. Another Tekakwitha Conference attendee, Rich May, also discussed the importance of her relic. Rich is a Catholic speaker and educator, providing lectures and workshops across the country and on television and radio. I interviewed him at the El Paso conference, and he mentioned that he wears Kateri's relic on a necklace, and at gatherings such as the conference, if he meets someone who has an affliction, he would loan the relic to that person to help them heal.

Rich's workshop at the conference in El Paso focused on the rosary. In his ministry to Native Americans, he saw a need to create educational materials that reflected the beauty of Native culture, thus he created booklets that teach about the rosary and feature Indigenous-themed artwork and connections to Indigenous cultural teachings, paralleling Mother Earth to Mother Mary, for example, and how we should love them both. When I asked Rich what his message about Saint Kateri to future generations would be, he responded that we should model Tekakwitha's spirituality: "You don't have to be a theologian to understand it, you can just have a very simple, but very well grounded [spirituality] ... she knew her priorities, so look at what Kateri's priorities were and make it your own." Rich keeps this message in mind as he prepares educational materials and presentations for his ministry efforts, many of which are greatly valued by Indigenous community members, as his workshops at the National Tekakwitha Conferences always attract a large audience. This section has shown diverse ways in which Indigenous peoples and non-Native allies build communities that help lift all peoples up, on the path of becoming real human beings. In the final section of this chapter, I reflect on the principles of community building that we have examined.

Conclusion: Principles of Community Building

In this chapter, we examined examples of Indigenous people and their non-Native allies building community by putting one's trust in the hands of the spirit powers. This work is deeply transformative for the people involved. It is also deeply connected to Indigenous cultural traditions, which teach us that humans are spiritual beings, manifested in a physical body. The examples discussed in this chapter demonstrate that Indigenous cultural teachings have within them the answers to our problems. The key lessons are: 1) *Interconnecting*: We are spiritual beings, and our physical health is connected to the spiritual well-being of our people. We must pray for ourselves, one another, and Mother Earth. 2) *Honoring*: We must care for ourselves and one another as spiritual beings; the ways in which we gather and celebrate community will have a deep impact on us, as we work toward a way of life that honors and celebrates all contributions people make. We can host inclusive events that affirm all members of the community are important; we can celebrate the rich histories of the land upon which we live, and we can celebrate traditions in ways that bring together multiple perspectives, yet continue to respect the Indigenous traditions of our lands. 3) *Embracing Responsibility*: We are all sacred, and we all have a role to play in building a healthy community. We need to seek out ways to bring people to community-building efforts, such as the Water Walk and the White Swan Summer Jam. 4) *Instructing*: Our cultural traditions are sacred instructions for living, which are given to us by the Creator.

I illustrate the principles of community building in figure 17. Community building is portrayed on the back of a turtle, inspired by Saint Kateri Tekakwitha's belonging to the Turtle Clan, as well as Sister Kateri Mitchell, who serves as a mentor and strong woman role model to many Indigenous peoples, including Sister Clissene. The four principles, summarized in figure 17, are drawn from the examples shared in this chapter: Interconnecting physical and spiritual health and well-being is shown in the Yakama examples, serving our traditional foods at spiritual gatherings, and providing spaces for families to engage in healthy exercise and community bonding. Honoring all peoples' contributions is shown in the inclusive approaches of the Yakama examples and the Water Walk. Embracing responsibility is demonstrated in all of the examples of community members stepping forward to provide ways for their communities to be healthier—whether it is showing leadership in providing a special gathering for Saint Mary's 125th Anniversary, helping hold the finish-line tape at community track meets, participating in walking and praying for the water, or dedicating oneself to creating a new religious order to serve Native peoples. Instructing is interwoven across the examples in this chapter, including Native men who draw from Indigenous cultural

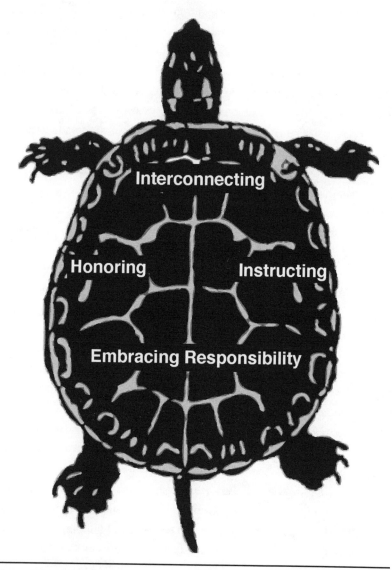

Figure 17 Four principles of community building. Credit: Michelle M. Jacob and Christopher J. Andersen.

teachings and ceremonies to guide their spiritual work with Indigenous communities, and religious clergy placing Indigenous cultural teachings and the devotion of Saint Kateri at the center of their community-building efforts.

Chapter 3 has shown there are many ways that one can embrace responsibility for helping to build a healthy community. We have explored ways that Indigenous peoples continue to draw from their cultural traditions in their community-building work. Catholic celebrations at Saint Mary's honor traditional Yakama spiritual teachings, linking us to the land and honoring the Creator's instructions to pray for the foods, which have sustained our peoples since time immemorial. Elders are revered as spiritual leaders and teachers during the opening prayers at the community track meets. Anishinaabe elders teach about traditions for caring for the water, and encourage women to reclaim their roles as caretakers. The grandmother teachings are serving as the basis for the community-building work of the Water Walks. Finally, Sister Clissene begins her spiritual journey of founding a new Catholic religious order by being blessed in Apache ways. These forms of prayer and cultural practice serve to strengthen all forms of community building. They also serve as a powerful inspiration to help guide non-Native allies into a Cycle of Healing discussed in chapter 1. This chapter has shown how men's dedication to Saint Kateri is important. We have also examined how non-Native allies benefit from Indigenous cultural teachings and, when they internalize the teachings, allies can also contribute to community building.

Indigenous cultural traditions can be upheld in "unexpected places," such as the Catholic Church sanctuary, the public school track, and in religious-order ministry formation and outreach. Across these diverse examples, we see the dynamic expressions and efforts of health and spirituality interwoven and lived in daily life of Indigenous peoples, and allies who work and live alongside Indigenous peoples on their homelands. While this chapter has shared several examples of upholding Indigenous traditions within Western institutions, in chapter 4 we will examine competing discourses that surround Kateri Tekakwitha, and we will grapple with the idea of colonialism as an "ongoing disaster" within Native communities. We will examine the "unspeakable violence" inflicted upon and within tribal communities, and analyze the multiple ways in which Indigenous people engage in resistance and decolonizing practices.

4

The Ecstasy of Saint Kateri

Native Feminism in the Catholic Church

Ethnographic Introduction: Raffling Saint Kateri

A small crowd gathered around a table. It was obviously a booth that was really interesting—so many of the National Tekakwitha Conference members had decided to cluster together to view whatever artwork or information was on the table. I stepped closer to the crowd. Ah, yes! There is my mother right in the middle of the hubbub. What was she doing? I stood on my tiptoes to get a better look. She had a pen and was writing on slips of paper. She had a determined look on her face, writing with intention, with her brow and mouth set with focus. Ah! It is a raffle table! I scanned the area near the table and saw beautiful artwork all around. One striking piece featured Saint Kateri in an impressive frame with a large number 5 taped onto the corner. Wow! How beautiful the Native woman saint is with the trees and lilies surrounding her. Her head glows with the inferred meaning of the holy crown of angels. She is adorned with a simple brown shawl and a fringed buckskin dress. It is an image that resonates with many tribal peoples. Kateri's beautiful dark hair is braided, as my own mother braided my hair when I was younger. I thought of how this holy Native woman, just twenty-four years old when she died, was an inspiration to us all, as we traveled from across Turtle Island to come together as a spiritual community here in Fargo,

North Dakota. I thought of how many Native youth have it within them to draw from their strengths to do something remarkable—to make an impact on so many lives, as Saint Kateri has done. I think about my own university students, many of whom are Saint Kateri's age. How they hear the story of Saint Kateri in my American Indian studies classes and we discuss the ways in which parts of her story are silenced—they become "unspeakable" forms of violence. She was, in some ways, an alienated youth. I think about how this often unspoken part of Kateri's narrative resonates with my teenage students. They, too, know what it is like to have a wish for one's life that is not "popular," and how one can have big dreams that are not encouraged by one's guardians or authority figures. Some of them know what it is like to lose loved ones to illness.

My mother is finished with her task. She moves away from the crowded area and I ask her, "What did you do?"

"I entered the raffle! First thing I did when I got here. I didn't even go to the registration booth to get my name tag yet!"

"Whoa! You are serious, huh? Gonna win some prizes in the raffle?" I said, glancing at all the beautiful artwork on display at the raffle booth area.

"No. Only one prize. I put all my tickets into the bucket for the Kateri portrait. She just spoke to me and I said to myself, 'I am going to win that beautiful artwork of Kateri! I put all my tickets into bucket number five.'"

"Okay, Mom," I said, with a hint of doubt in my voice, as I stared at the already huge pile of raffle entries in the Kateri portrait bucket. I sensed many people would be entering the drawing for her, although there were several entries for the portraits of Pope John Paul II, Jesus, and Mary, among others.

Two days later, the raffle drawing was held during the dinner in the large ballroom of the conference center. The raffle prizes went one by one, until they got to the fifth prize, which I knew was the portrait of Saint Kateri, remembering the large "5" taped on to the beautiful work of art every time we walked past the raffle table over the past three days. Out of the corner of my eye, I could see my mother sitting tall with her best posture, and I wondered if she was praying to win. She whispered to remind me to go up and collect the portrait if she won, because it was too heavy for her. I said, "Yes, I know, you've already reminded me," and laughed a little bit, delighting in her raffle-winning confidence.

Figure 18 Kateri's portrait and raffle prize. Credit: Christopher J. Andersen.

Sure enough, the announcer boomed my mother's name over the ballroom speakers. I continued to laugh and smile on my way up to the announcer, and was congratulated by many of the conference attendees as I delicately wove my way in between crowded tables and chairs. When I reached the front of the room, the announcer said, "Congratulations! It is a beautiful picture of Saint Pope John Paul II. Go to the table and collect it now. They are waiting."

I smiled at the announcer, knowing he was mistaken, as Kateri had the "5" taped on her, not Pope John Paul II. My mother's heart was captivated by the beautiful portrayal of Kateri. I knew she would not enter the drawing for the photo of the elderly pope, hunched over and looking like he carried the weight of the world on his shoulders. I went to the table and collected the huge framed artwork of Kateri, giving the volunteer the matching raffle ticket for the fifth prize. Kateri's portrait, in the massive ornate frame, was heavy. But I managed, thanked the volunteers, and walked back to our place in the dining area. All along the way people stopped me and admired the image. They congratulated me (us) on winning it, while some spoke with mock fierce jealousy that they hadn't won. Even a Brother, in his brown Friar's robe, who was sitting at our dinner table, mock-threatened to steal the beautiful artwork. Everybody admired the magnificent representation of Saint Kateri. The artwork represented something sacred to all of us, as each conference attendee is devoted to the holy Indigenous woman in the painting I held in my hands.

After dinner, as I picked up the artwork, my mother and I were walking out of the dining area to prepare for the next session. A woman stopped us and told us the artist was her friend, and had a vendor table at the conference. We talked with this woman, Clementine, who described where the table was. We thanked her and proceeded to the table. The artist, Nellie Edwards, was delighted to meet us. We learned she was from the Yakima Valley, but lived in North Dakota. I asked her to sign the back of the painting. She humbly agreed.

Healing from Historical Trauma

Indigenous peoples still struggle to gain rights over our bodies, lands, and histories. Throughout Indian Country, there is an ongoing call to heal our people from the traumas of settler colonialism, which Dian Million describes as "a painful dismembering of families and societies" (2013, 20). Million uses a Native feminist analysis to understand the importance of Indigenous women's activism to bring about healing and justice for Indigenous peoples, and to critique the settler colonial powers, which continue to reap the benefits of conquest. Million accurately discusses the narratives of Indigenous healing as a cautionary tale. She defines the dangers involved: "In both Canada and the United States, at the same moment that we work to 'heal' we are also continuously assailed by the ongoing damages that are wreaked by racism, gender violence, political powerlessness, and the continuing breakdown of our affective networks, our communities, and our families" (ibid., 20). Million's cautionary tale reminds us that while Indigenous peoples continue to draw from traditions and kinship networks, which have helped our people survive for thousands of years, we are doing so within a settler colonial context that undermines such efforts. Colonialism is an ongoing process, and Indigenous communities are facing multiple traumas from historic and contemporary efforts to "develop" Indigenous lands. These settler colonial interventions are rooted in a long history of contact and conquest, and are tied to the missionary colonialism that was foundational in establishing settler colonial nation-states (Tinker 1993, Tinker 2014, Driskill, Finley, Gilley, and Morgensen 2011).

This chapter analyzes the competing narratives that surround one particular Indigenous woman, Saint Kateri Tekakwitha. I discuss the ongoing effects of settler colonial logics and Indigenous resistance to them, as Indigenous peoples find new ways of grappling with the "painful dismembering" that Million articulated. Throughout the master narratives of history, Kateri's virginity, femininity, and indigeneity are fantasized as part of an ongoing settler colonial project that seeks to delegitimize women's powerful roles within Indigenous communities. I argue that through this process: 1) Indigenous sexuality is censored, while settler colonial heteropatriarchy is upheld; 2) religion is used as a tool to establish and maintain dichotomies that portray Indigenous peoples as either "traditional" or "Christian"; 3) settler colonialism is a transhistoric phenomenon that constructs Indigenous peoples, lands, and cultures as inherently rapable, thus connecting the violence of the 1600s that Kateri witnessed to the contemporary forms of violence that continue to "painfully dismember" Indigenous communities today; and 4) Indigenous peoples and allies resist the Cycle of Destruction in powerful ways, and implement a Cycle of Healing within their lives and their communities.

Saint Kateri Tekakwitha was born to a Mohawk chief and an Algonquin Christian mother. Her mother was adopted and recognized as a full member of Mohawk society. Tekakwitha grew up in the traditional Mohawk longhouse culture and was recognized for her outstanding skills as a craft worker, making beautiful baskets and wampum belts. Her father was a traditionalist and resisted the influx of colonists and missionaries, perhaps foreseeing the devastation they would bring to his people. Tekakwitha's parents and brother were killed in the smallpox epidemic that swept through her village in 1660, when Tekakwitha was just four years old (Vecsey 2012). Tekakwitha also became very ill with smallpox, but survived, although she was badly scarred from pockmarks and her eyesight was very poor for the rest of her life. Orphaned, Tekakwitha was taken in by her uncle's family, and raised as their daughter. Her uncle was strongly opposed to a missionary presence in their village, seeking to protect the culture, traditions, and health of his people. Various accounts state that Tekakwitha was interested in Christianity, and perhaps her mother had taught her some initial teachings about Christ. Despite her uncle's protest, missionaries visited their village and Tekakwitha became more interested in the Catholic religion. Ultimately, she left her home village and moved to Saint Peter's Mission near Montreal, which was a "site for gathering in potential converts and neophyte Christians under clerical rule, set apart from undue influences, both French and Native" (Vecsey 2012, 14).

Tekakwitha demonstrated intense devotion, amazing the French and Native peoples alike. She was baptized with the Christian name "Catherine," after Saint Catherine of Siena. Her name is most commonly spelled "Kateri," approximating a Mohawk spelling of her Christian name. Kateri Tekakwitha was revered in the praying village for her extreme devotion and spiritual practice. She self-flagellated frequently, often to the point of exhaustion and illness. She demonstrated an extreme self-discipline that both startled and amazed the French missionaries, who looked to Kateri as an inspiration (Greer 2005). Kateri used her body to assert her control over her life, and she used it as a tool to exercise her spiritual devotion. While Catholic narratives celebrate docile virginal young women's bodies, Kateri herself was perhaps anything but docile, as she ruthlessly tortured her body; she was committed to strict penance, demonstrating a fierce willpower and tolerance of pain. The French Jesuits wrote about Kateri's "saintly" devotion during her lifetime, and after her death, the writings intensified. Many of Kateri's devotees already regarded Kateri as a saint, but they had to wait until 2012 to witness her official canonization by the Roman Catholic Church.

I met Jack Casey, one of Kateri's followers, at the canonization event at the Vatican in 2012. Jack, an Irish-Catholic lawyer and writer from Albany, New York, made the journey to Rome because he had been devoted to Kateri for thirty years (Casey 2012). In my interview with him, Jack stated that Kateri had helped him in times of crisis in his life, beginning in his early adulthood,

I was a young father, I was just starting practicing law, and I feel that she got me over the threshold in both of those enterprises . . . I've had a lot of turmoil in my life and I think that she has been a guiding spirit . . . when the canonization was announced last December I was going through a terrible crisis and it came at the exact moment that I needed something to believe in. . . . She was a pivotal figure when an awful lot of imperialism and ethnic cleansing and genocide and all those really horrible things were going on in the area where I'm from, Albany, New York. And she survived. Not only did she survive, but she embraced the God of her persecutors in such a way that she became admirable to them . . . what I admire most is her iron will . . . she decided what was important to her.

Jack has devoted himself to Kateri, and he credits the holy Indigenous woman with consistently helping him through difficult times. When I interviewed him about Kateri's influence in his life, he articulated that her model of strength and faith was deeply inspiring to him, and helped him understand the history of his local surroundings in upstate New York, thus providing him a deeper connection to the Mohawk homeland where he resides.

While many of Kateri's followers celebrated her canonization as an affirmation of Indigenous peoples' importance within the Church, other questions remain about Indigenous feminine representation within the Church, and in society more broadly. What does Kateri, as a symbol, have to teach us about the legacy of settler colonial history and Indigenous peoples' responses to it? Does Kateri's importance transcend a sort of tokenistic "politics of recognition" within the settler colonial Church, which remains committed to dispossessing Indigenous peoples (Coulthard 2014)? Does she represent a mere attempt to "neutralize" colonial violence (Tinker 2014)? How does Kateri open up new spaces and opportunities to define and reclaim Native femininity as part of spiritual practice? To address these concerns, I analyze examples of Catholic Church–sanctioned literature about Saint Kateri, and I draw from primary interviews and ethnographic fieldwork among contemporary Indigenous peoples and Kateri devotees. In doing so, I offer a Native feminist analysis of the multiple narratives that surround Saint Kateri, including the unspeakable violence of settler colonialism within Catholic master narratives, the inherent rapability of Indigenous peoples, lands, and cultures within settler colonial logics, and the importance of Indigenous resistance, which reclaims the Indigenous feminine as sacred. I conclude the chapter with a discussion of the ways Kateri's kin, contemporary Mohawk peoples, are struggling to protect their homeland and reclaim their cultural traditions in the face of widespread corporate pollution of their land, water, and bodies. Their resistance to protect Mohawk homeland is especially fitting given that Kateri is the patron saint of "people who love nature, work in ecology, and preserve the natural and human environments" (Walker 2012).

Virgin Forests and a Virgin Mohawk Maiden

Largely written by Catholics, and mostly by Jesuits, there has been a nearly constant stream of literature written about Kateri Tekakwitha, fantasizing her femininity, sexuality, and indigeneity. During Kateri's life, the French Jesuits were amazed by her strong self-discipline, and they admired her ability to endure strict penance. Across the centuries, Catholic narratives glorify Kateri as a devout Catholic virgin who "took Christ as her bridegroom." This language incorporates Kateri, as a celibate woman, into a heteropatriarchal system, even though she chose not to be in sexual relationships with men. Additionally, for Native women there are also racial and cultural implications undermining Indigenous collectivism and empowerment. For example, Mohawk author Darren Bonaparte analyzes the contested imagery that surrounds Saint Kateri: "When another [white, Catholic] culture took one of our women, turned her into an icon, and placed her on a pedestal, many of her own people turned their back on her" (Bonaparte 2009, 268). Bonaparte's analysis calls attention to the diversity of views within Indigenous communities, and the contested meanings surrounding Saint Kateri are an example of this. To the extent that she represents an empowered vision for Indigenous peoples, she tends to be embraced. But when Saint Kateri is articulated as a "savage" who was "saved" because she left her people and culture, then her symbolism becomes deeply problematic for Indigenous peoples. Bonaparte also notes that although Kateri is perhaps the most well-known

Mohawk woman and the Church gloriously upholds her, it is ironic that, because of her celibacy, she is not a direct ancestor to any living Mohawk peoples (Bonaparte 2009). In addition to this lack of biological regeneration, her celibacy is framed, in Catholic narratives, as grounded in her devout worship of a white Christ whose teachings were taught to her by French Jesuit male missionaries. The Catholic master narratives undermine Native feminine agency; in them, Kateri is not portrayed as a woman who could pick and choose her destiny from a variety of options available in Mohawk and New France societies. Instead, she is portrayed as a young woman who was reacting to an oppressive uncle, and fleeing to safety, living under French Jesuit men. The tidy placement of Kateri into a settler colonial heteropatriarchal order denies Kateri the agency of a woman who is drawing from her cultural teachings, which define women as strong decision-makers (Shoemaker 1995).

The master narratives within Catholic writings about Kateri enforce a strict "either/or" dichotomy of Indigenous peoples as "either" devoted to Christ "or" heathen savages. For example, Edward LaMore's Catholic Church–sanctioned historical play portrays Kateri as "overcoming" her tribal background and identity to "blossom" into something beautiful and spiritual. As mentioned in chapter 1, LaMore refers to Kateri as being "like a lily in a mud pond or a daisy in a coal mine," and states she came from the "worst imaginable environment" but transcended this horrible condition to be a model of "piety and saintliness" (LaMore 1932). Such discourse perpetuates the ideas of Indigenous cultures and peoples as savage, worthy of conquering, and void of spiritual strengths; it is a narrative that dehumanizes Indigenous peoples and renders their homeland, Mother Earth, as a wild but conquerable commodity that should be tamed by colonizing masters.

LaMore's play also draws from a settler colonial discourse, which portrays Indigenous peoples in a vanquished but romantic fashion. That is, once the savages have been conquered, it is acceptable to speak of them romantically, and doing so perpetuates what Tinker calls the "romantic colonialist narratives," which "casts the genocidal devastation of Indian peoples as an unfortunate but necessary tragedy" (Tinker 2014, 5). In his front-matter dedication to his play, LaMore describes Kateri, her homeland, and her people romantically. LaMore states that his work is dedicated to Kateri, whom he describes as "the fairest flower that ever blossomed in our virgin forests and to the honor of her brave race that once peopled our hills and valleys, our forests and streams" (LaMore 1932, 6). A "brave race" is certainly distinct from the "mud pond" or "coal mine" descriptors that are used elsewhere in the book to describe Kateri's "heathen" cultural background. Nevertheless, Kateri's forested homeland is described as "virgin," and LaMore asserts the settler colonial ownership of the land, claiming the virgin forests as "ours" along with the hills, valleys, forests, and streams—the brave race is now vanquished and the colonial project is implied as successfully complete. Within this framework of sexualizing landscapes, when the virgin forests are firmly under settler colonial control, they are transformed into something economically productive for empire and white settlers, as opposed to the "worst imaginable environment," which describes Mohawk homeland before being conquered. The settler colonial logic has clear implications: when Indigenous peoples are in charge, it is a terrible environment; when white settlers are in charge, it is a land of beautiful virgin forests. Such colonial logics uphold the abjection of Indigenous peoples, as Tinker argues, because "colonialism only works when the colonizer first of all rationalizes his superiority and normativity over [and] against those he has colonized or displaced" (Tinker 2014, 18).

Settler colonial views of Indigenous homeland are, of course, framed quite differently than Indigenous understandings of homeland. LaMore's play can be understood as an expression of the ecstasy of having power over Mohawk virgin hills, valleys, forests, and streams, and the taming and co-optation of Kateri into a neatly defined settler colonial heteropatriarchal order. In Catholic master narratives, Kateri's rejection of marriage is not framed as a rejection of settler colonial gender norms. Thus, the lasting lesson that surrounds Kateri in the master narratives of the Catholic Church is one that promotes a virginal Indigenous woman who craves the civilizing influence of the Church, and thus she mirrors the virgin lands that must also be wrangled into submission and civilized by the settler colonial apparatus.

However, Indigenous peoples contest the settler colonial view of Kateri and her homeland. For example, Mohawk author Darren Bonaparte rejects the idea that traditional Mohawk villages are "the worst imaginable environment" for leading a good and saintly life. In his text about traditional Mohawk culture, history, and spirituality, in which he calls for a Mohawk repatriation of Kateri Tekakwitha, Bonaparte argues that many of the traits Catholic missionaries praised in Kateri were indeed lessons she learned as part of traditional matriarchal Mohawk longhouse culture (2009). Bonaparte notes, "In more than just name, the old bark longhouse is at the very heart of our identity . . . one could not live in such close confines without a 'Great Law of Peace'" (Bonaparte 2009, 69). Tekakwitha, through her dedicated work on traditional crafts, arts, and material culture, embodied the traditional teachings. She fulfilled important duties and had an important place in traditional Mohawk society because of her gifts.

Historical-cultural accuracy and understanding is not the central concern in the Catholic literature about Kateri Tekakwitha. In LaMore's play, he writes a love scene that features Tekakwitha, who has refused to marry an Indigenous man. In the dramatic love scene, which takes place in the area near Tekakwitha's Mohawk village, LaMore writes,

> Tekakwitha hears a flute playing the Mohawk love song. She hears it from far off in the forest, and then sings the love song to God (although she is not sure what to call Him). Her cousins find her and start teasing her because they saw a young man playing the flute song and believed Tekakwitha was singing to him. She denies it and says, "No, I think you do not know Him! He is not known to many of our people. [*With enthusiasm.*] My lover is a powerful chieftain. His lodge is large and beautiful. In it there is always peace and contentment, warmth and happiness. About it roam the animals of the forest, the deer, the elk, the buffalo, and the turkey. His streams are crystal-like and abound with fish. His kingdom is very great and His tribesmen numerous. He is kind, generous, and tender with his love. I love Him. I sang my love song to Him. (LaMore 1932, 44)

In the scene, Kateri is described as being "in love" with God. Although she is portrayed as claiming God/Him/Jesus as her lover, she does not know his name. Tekakwitha's cousins tease her about an assumed Mohawk lover, but Tekakwitha denies feeling love for her Mohawk suitors and is staunchly opposed to marriage with a Mohawk man. In LaMore's play, Kateri refers to God as her "lover" and says He is a "powerful chieftain" with a "big lodge" where there is always warmth, happiness, and buffalo. It is notable that Kateri here lists the riches of the Creator's gifts to her people. She lists the meat and fish that are plentiful.

Perhaps then, there could have been an opening in LaMore's work to discuss the importance of an Indigenous traditional ecological framework. According to Indigenous teachings, the Creator instructed the people how to take care of one another and the land. Such a discussion could have linked the health of the people to the health of their land, water, culture, and traditions. However, this traditional Indigenous perspective is left out of the discourse. Also remaining unspoken in the play is a critique of the dramatic social, economic, and political shift that disempowered Mohawk peoples, as the settler colonial powers brought havoc to Tekakwitha's people. Thus, left out of LaMore's play is the awareness and articulation of what Nicole Guidotti-Hernández calls "unspeakable violence" of settler colonialism (2011). The smallpox epidemic brought by settlers, which scarred young Tekakwitha's body, took her eyesight, and left her an orphan, is glossed over, as are the ways in which Indigenous peoples were used as pawns in wars and land struggles among the French, Dutch, British (and later the United States and Canada)—all of which served as what Andrea Smith describes as a raping of Indigenous people's lands and cultures (2005a). These same colonial powers devastated the land and cultural resources of Tekakwitha's people.

LaMore does not ponder why the beloved animals of the forest were not in abundance after settler colonial encounters. Nor does he deal with why Mohawk peoples might be struggling to find "peace and contentment, warmth and happiness." Mohawk scholar Darren Bonaparte critiques the master narratives of history because they are part of "scorched earth tactics" that destroy Mohawk peoples and cultures. Bonaparte notes that "genocidal acts are footnotes in history today. In fact, few Mohawks today are even aware that it happened," even though the colonial powers had repeatedly sought to "wipe us from the face of the earth forever" (Bonaparte 2009, 118). Historian David Chang articulates that the settler colonial relationship to land was one that sought enclosure, and a dramatic shift of power from Indigenous peoples to the nation-state. This ultimately established a settler colonial "regime of property and power" (Chang 2011, 117). All of these forms of colonial violence destroyed Indigenous families, cultures, economies, and gender norms (Tuck and Yang 2012).

Loss of Women's Powerful Roles

The historical master narrative in Catholic literature deemphasizes women's powerful roles in Mohawk society; settler colonial violence sought to destroy traditional Indigenous gender norms. Bonaparte confirms that Mohawk traditional culture is matriarchal, with women not only choosing who would serve as their chief, but also having the greatest influence over the chief (Bonaparte 2009). Bonaparte questions why Kateri is described in the Catholic narratives as being "awakened" from a supposed "darkness" and "slumber" of her traditional culture, and contests the portrayal of Tekakwitha as special *because* of her *differentness* from her Indigenous kin (2009, 71). Bonaparte argues that when the French Jesuits describe Kateri in their writings, and praise her strengths, "they describe a child going about her life like anyone else, participating in work and recreational activities the same as other Mohawk girls. In fact, they say that she was a particularly gifted artisan with a deft touch. As much as they try to convey that she was somehow alien to it, she was a part of her culture, and a valued one at that" (ibid., 71).

Kateri's power in the Catholic narratives derives from her subservience to Jesus Christ; however, it is done in a way that portrays Kateri so that she fits neatly within the settler colonial heteropatriarchal order. Other scholars have written about the ways in which Christianity has upset traditional Indigenous gender norms, which historically have afforded women power and importance within Indigenous societies. Heteropatriarchy is a logic used to perpetuate violence against women in general, and Indigenous women in particular. Christianity continues to perpetuate this settler colonial logic by upholding sexism in Christian churches and destroying traditional Indigenous practices as part of the Christian settler colonial mission (Smith 2006, 2008).

Native feminist scholarship analyzes the ways in which violence is naturalized against women, as well as Indigenous homelands and sacred sites, oftentimes pointing out how religious and state institutions work together to perpetuate settler colonial violence, which disempowers Native communities. Winona LaDuke has written about the ongoing conflict over Mt. Graham in Arizona, and how the Vatican is a major player in land dispossession and denial of access to sacred sites for Indigenous peoples (LaDuke 2005). In his writings about Mt. Graham, Joel Helfrich also critiques the Vatican's role in refusing to view the sacred mountain as a site that should not be developed. Helfrich details the activism of Apache elder Ola Cassadore Davis, noting that Ola "was outraged by the role of the Vatican, especially the Pope, in the astrophysical development: 'He should understand about religion . . . and that mountain is important to the traditional religion of my people'" (Helfrich 2014). Mt. Graham is a sacred site to Indigenous peoples in the southwestern United States, including Apache peoples who pilgrimage to the Mt. Graham area to hold important spiritual ceremonies, such as the coming of age ceremony for girls. Yet, the University of Arizona and the Vatican have collaborated to erect a large telescope and observatory facility on Mt. Graham to learn more about the heavens. Apaches must now navigate a bureaucratic system to obtain, in advance, a permit to pray at their sacred site in which they honor girls in their transformation into healthy young women. Thus, the timeless ceremony for Apache peoples, and women in particular, to ensure a healthy, spiritually grounded process for becoming the life bearers of the next generation is now disrupted by state and religious institutions who insist they know what is best for the sacred land. In this way, Indigenous peoples, cultures, and lands continue to be inherently rapable, as Andrea Smith (2005a) articulates—from a Native feminist perspective. Nation-states and Christian institutions continue to be bedfellows in the ongoing settler colonial project, to have their way with Indigenous homelands: mounting telescopes, denying access to pray at sacred sites, and implementing bureaucratic paperwork processes for the "right" to pray at sacred sites, the rights to which are sold to the highest bidder to do as they please.

The settler colonial gendered order not only displaces the power of Native women, but Native men are also demeaned. For example, within the Catholic narratives, Kateri is portrayed as running away from her village to escape the religious persecution of her uncle, who did not welcome missionary settlement in the village. Native men are portrayed as "heathen" and are a limitation to be "overcome." Kateri's uncle is portrayed as a brute who wishes to deny Kateri the right to worship Christ; so surely a damning future is in store for him. Bonaparte offers a counternarrative, however, insisting that readers should consider what any father/uncle figure would do if his young daughter/niece wanted to leave her family to live among strange men in a faraway land. The settler colonial logic of demonizing Native men and seeking to "protect" Native women from their disordered people is one that continues to structure the ways in which issues of gender violence are viewed, and has an impact on how legal/political/medical institutions distribute (or withhold) resources. Oftentimes, as Native feminist scholars point out, Native women are portrayed as victims who need to be protected from the violence within their communities, a view that has the ill effect of disempowering Native women and criminalizing Native men, and suggests that more surveillance of Native communities (by law enforcement/corrections officers, social workers, mental health professionals) is the answer (Million 2013, Smith 2005a).

The colonizing portrayal of Native men (as savages) and Native women (as victims) does not fit with traditional Indigenous cultural teachings, many of which are explicitly based on gender equality. In my work with Wynona Peters, we argue that gender inequality was introduced, enforced, and naturalized within Indigenous communities as a main part of the settler colonial project, although male tribal leaders resisted such ploys to undermine Indigenous women's importance as laborers and traditional holders of wealth within Indigenous communities (Jacob and Peters 2011). The settler colonial apparatus expected Native men who served as tribal leaders/chiefs to side with the white men who sought to control Native women. Yet, Native men instead supported Native women and denied having control over them, or the right to assert control over Native women. These patterns of leadership, rooted in traditional Indigenous cultures, affirm the importance of Native women as active subjects, whose membership and representation within communities is understood and supported (ibid.). Native women did not need "protection" or "surveillance" to be safe within their traditional communities.

Disrupting Settler Colonial Logics: Native Feminism in the Catholic Church

It is perhaps not surprising that the master narratives of Kateri Tekakwitha are soiled with the sexism and heteropatriarchy of settler colonial logics. However, these are not the only representations of Saint Kateri. For generations, Indigenous women have presented counternarratives of the beloved Indigenous woman. All across the United States, Indigenous communities continue to be served by Catholic mission churches, and many of these churches have priests who understand the importance of respectful representation of Indigenous peoples and cultures, including Saint Kateri. Many of these priests celebrate Mass dressed in garments that feature Saint Kateri as a strong and beautiful subject, using imagery created by Indigenous women themselves. In this way, the priests use their bodies to show respect for the Indigenous woman who inspires such devotion from her followers. I witnessed one such example at the Saint Regis Mohawk Mission Church at the Akwesasne Mohawk Reservation, which sits on Mohawk homeland at the intersection of what is now upstate New York, southern Quebec, and southern Ontario. Akwesasne homeland is beautiful, surrounded by the rolling foothills and Adirondack Mountains, along with the life-giving rivers, including the Saint Regis and Saint Lawrence, which flow nearby. It is sacred Indigenous homeland that has sustained the people for countless generations. Around the river bend, however, lie huge aluminum plants, and their eerie presence haunts the landscape. Yet, the people survive and thrive on their homeland because of an unshakable sense of the importance of community and culture. Mohawk women, who pray to Saint Kateri every day, care for the Mission Church. At the Mass, the mission priest adorns his body with the Kateri vestment, and he visually becomes a holy man who understands the need to remember and respect the centrality of Mohawk women on this homeland. His vestment was a gift from the Mohawk women who do much of the work caring for the church and community. In my focus group with Mohawk women, they explained the importance of culture and spirituality, and insisted that traditional culture is central to the expression of all forms of spirituality, including Catholicism.

Figure 19 Indigenous choir sings in Mohawk at the Mass of Thanksgiving for Kateri's Canonization inside St. Peter's Basilica at the Vatican. Credit: Michelle M. Jacob.

Women discussed the importance of sharing traditional cultural teachings with children, and this love for their community inspired many forms of activism, including the establishment of the Akwesasne Freedom School, where their traditional culture, including Mohawk language, is taught and valued. The women viewed culture and Catholic spiritual expression as interwoven, and talked about teaching children hymns in Mohawk, wearing traditional regalia to celebrate the Holy Mass, and bringing traditional dances into the church. They recorded a CD of hymns sung in Mohawk in a collection titled, "Enska Tsi Teionkwarihwakwen" (One in the Spirit). On another CD they recorded, "TEION KWARI WAKON: Selections of Mohawk Hymns," the women stated, "We are so thankful to our parents, grandparents, aunties, and former choir members for teaching us these hymns and encouraging us to carry on singing in our language. It is our hope that our younger people will pick it up and our tradition of singing hymns in our language will be learned and carried on" (Akwesasne Mohawk Wake

Choir 2006). Their hope has been fulfilled, as hymns have been a powerful way that Mohawk language continues to be learned and shared, including within the celebration of Mass. During the 2012 canonization ceremony for Kateri Tekakwitha at the Vatican, songs were sung in Mohawk. The choir, led by Indigenous artist Marcus Briggs-Cloud, performed beautifully at the canonization ceremony, and in the Mass of Thanksgiving the day after the canonization, a Mass was held inside of Saint Peter's Basilica and was exclusively open to the pilgrims who had traveled to Rome to honor Tekakwitha.

The priest at the mission church at Akwesasne had a beautiful vestment that honored Kateri. He received the vestment as a gift from the Mohawk women who care for the community and for the mission church at Saint Regis. The Kateri vestment was itself an Indigenous transnational tie to

Figure 20 Wynona Peters, in regalia, at the Mass of Thanksgiving (with author). Credit: Christopher J. Andersen.

other Native women who honor Kateri. The Mohawk women bought the Kateri vestment from two Navajo women elders, who design and sew clergy vestments as their small business in their retirement years. Their business is called Native Blessing Way (named in honor of the Navajo/Diné Blessing Way ceremony) and is owned and operated by Vi Blackman and Hazel Jendritza, two sisters who sew the garments out of love for the Native woman saint, Kateri, and because they have pride in their Indigenous culture and spirituality. They, too, insist traditional Indigenous culture is not at odds with Catholic teachings. They reject the either/or dichotomy—that one is either "traditional" or "Christian"—that underlies the narratives of conquest within Christianity and the nation-state (Treat 1996, Tinker 1993).

Vi and Hazel shared that Kateri helps to guide them on the spiritual path to sew garments honoring Indigenous cultural arts traditions. I interviewed Vi and Hazel at the 74th Annual National Tekakwitha Conference in El Paso, Texas, in 2013. Their work represents an Indigenous artistic expression that places Indigenous culture and people at the center of a Catholic identity. Hazel explained that her sister, Vi, introduced her to the National Tekakwitha Conference. She became involved in volunteering and sponsoring the conference when it was held in her area, Tucson, in 2005. Hosting the conference is a three-year process, with two years of planning before the conference takes place. Hazel learned in the process that the main emphases are learning to be a role model—living like Kateri as a humble woman caring for the people—coming together with Indigenous peoples across the country, and renewing old friendships with people. Hazel is inspired to follow in Kateri's footsteps by loving people and not getting distracted by "being busy" in life. Hazel shared the following narrative with me:

> She's our role model. And she's Native . . . and my sister is my role model, too, because she is a very spiritual woman and has encouraged me to do a lot. Because I wasn't very active . . . since then I've just been very busy . . . with our ministry sewing vestments. She [Kateri] is looking at me in this image. She is there . . . spiritually. I talk to her. . . . When we heard that she was going to be canonized I just got goose bumps all over. Oh my gosh! It is really coming about! I didn't think we would see it in our lifetime . . . maybe all of our prayers [for Kateri's canonization] helped . . . fortunately we were able to see

Figure 21 Hazel and Vi at the 2013 National Tekakwitha Conference in El Paso, Texas. Credit: Michelle M. Jacob.

it happen. . . . One of my younger sisters . . . she has a lot of health issues . . . we also give her the images and pictures of Kateri and she is becoming a very spiritual person because of Kateri. . . . The rest of my family, they know . . . what we are about . . . miracles are not impossible. They happen. . . . She [Kateri] was living with her Native beliefs, but that basically is what it is, is we embrace both, Catholic faith and Western culture and whatever we do. Like I was a nurse and all these things all go together and make you a better person . . . our business name, Native Blessing Way, that is part of our Navajo culture. We have Native Blessing Ways to cure us and restore us if we are out of balance. Looking at Blessing Way . . . I was a nurse and a nurse mid-wife. I know all my patients, in their third trimester would have Blessing Way prayers and basically we would pray for safe delivery, a well child, the whole pregnancy would turn out well. And I know if you leave the reservation, sometimes they do the Blessing Way to live in harmony . . . embrace all of it. It makes you a better person . . . Kateri is our role model, she is a saint, and that is what we should strive to do, whatever we do, wherever we are. We don't have to do anything special . . . shouldn't be judgmental, just accept people the way they are. And I think you have to role model that. You don't treat other people right; they pick up on that. My daughter and nieces and nephews . . . I want them to respect each other. Those are the qualities that God instilled in us . . . . Just word of mouth . . . we are able to develop our business through the conference and I guess it would be the intercession of Kateri and that helps us with our business . . . the main thing is the designing and that is what my sister does. And we work together very well . . . our Native values . . . it was a natural thing . . . we look to my dad for our traditional teachings because our grandfather was a medicine man. So my dad always talked about our Native culture and how we embrace it. It wasn't contrary to our Catholic faith. My mother was the devout Catholic. We sit back here now and think about it. We do a lot of talking and remember things when we were young. And they make impressions on us, why our parents were telling us certain things and it helps us be a better person.

These tribal elders model Native women's empowerment through their collaborative work together, as they care for one another and create art that honors Kateri. Hazel discusses the ways in which her parents taught her to draw from both her Indigenous and Catholic traditions so as to live to her fullest ability. She discusses the ways in which she and her sister reflect on the meaning and importance of the lessons that their parents shared with them. Their work and the way in which they conduct themselves demonstrate the power and importance of the teachings of the Blessing Way. Diné scholar Lloyd Lee explains, "The Blessing Way is the backbone of all Diné ceremonies. The ceremony is the happiest and most harmonious and peaceful ritual. The Blessing Way is a mechanism to secure a person's path" (Lee 2014, 6). The primary way that Hazel and Vi choose to live out their Indigenous Catholicism today is through their devotion to Kateri, who brings them to a better life, a stronger form of spirituality. They carry out important ministry work in their business, Native Blessing Way, traveling around the country and meeting Indigenous people and clergy, sharing the Kateri vestments and selling them. In doing so, they place an Indigenous woman at the center of Catholic ceremony. Their vestments, adorned with Indigenous-inspired designs and artwork, complement Saint Kateri's image, which is the focal point of the artwork. Vi designs all the vestments; she shared with me that Kateri inspires her, and doing the work is a blessing, a way of living prayer. In their work, Vi and Hazel affirm the importance of Native women-centered spirituality. They lovingly create the vestments that priests wear to celebrate Mass. In doing so, they share the importance of Kateri. This work resists the settler colonial logic, which defines Native peoples as "vanished" and Native cultures as "dead." By reclaiming the importance of Native women and cultures, Vi and Hazel share their Blessing Way approach with each other, tribal community members, and clergy. By expressing strong Native women-centered subjectivity, they help define Native femininity as strong, collaborative, and rooted in Native traditions, insisting they are not at odds with Catholicism.

In Hazel's quotation, she explains that Kateri is inspiring because she lived with her Native ways. Hazel and Vi follow Kateri's example by placing their traditional Navajo spiritual teachings at the center of their practice. As Hazel explained, her grandfather's teachings as a medicine man, and her father's traditional teachings, complemented the spiritual teachings that their mother shared through her Catholic practice. In combining their spiritual practices and beliefs, such as the Navajo Blessing Way, and their devotion to Kateri in sewing the vestments to be used in the Holy Mass, Vi and Hazel disrupt the settler colonial narratives of Native women as passive objects, and thoroughly reject the either/or dichotomy of traditional/heathen versus Catholic/human.

Vi and Hazel offer us an alternative view of Native women and Kateri's role within the Catholic Church. In their view, she is the inspiration for celebrating Indigenous spirituality; Kateri offers a way to reclaim a Native woman figure as central to spiritual practice. Other Indigenous peoples draw similar inspiration, and remake the physical space of Catholic churches as part of their spiritual expression. For example, the Kateri Tekakwitha Circle on the Yakama Reservation celebrates Saint Kateri's feast day in July. At the

Figure 22 Altar at the Yakama Kateri Circle Celebration of Saint Kateri's Feast Day in 2013. Credit: Michelle M. Jacob.

2013 celebration, the mission church on the reservation was adorned with images of Kateri, included prominently in front of the altar.

One of the leaders and tribal elders in the Yakama Reservation Kateri Circle, Lydia Johnson (Yakama/Cayuse), said, "this seventeenth century Mohawk woman of faith is an example of how God has always had a relationship with the First Peoples of this continent, has always recognized their spirituality and faith despite post-contact pronouncements from his European-American followers that Indigenous people were heathens" (Walker 2012). Lydia rejects the settler colonial logics that portray Indigenous peoples as heathens, and insists God has "always" recognized Indigenous spirituality and faith. Lydia's narrative disrupts the assumptions that Indigenous peoples are void of spirituality and ignorant of God. Traditional Yakama teachings affirm Lydia's narrative; tribal teachings articulate that the Creator placed Yakama peoples on our homeland and gifted us with our traditional foods and language. Our culture is sacred; our peoplehood and continuing cultural practices are evidence of our blessed relationship with the Creator (Uebelacker 1984, Yakima Indian Nation Tribal Council 1977, Jacob 2013). Many people on the Yakama reservation combine traditional teachings with contemporary Christian practices. Lydia is president of the board of directors of the Yakama Reservation–based Northwest Kateri Tekakwitha Spiritual Center, a nonprofit organization that will build a community center in Lydia's hometown of Wapato, Washington, on the Yakama Reservation on five acres of land that Lydia donated. Through her leadership in this organization, Lydia upholds a traditional teaching of caring for the people and working collaboratively with one's community. The community spiritual center is an expression of these ideals; it represents what I call Native feminism in practice. Lydia shows her love for the community and devotion to Kateri by donating her own ancestral plot of land as the site for the Kateri center. She uses the gift from the Creator, our homeland, as part of her spiritual practice.

Tekakwitha's example as a strong Native feminine, spiritual role model inspires so many Indigenous women. For example, Geneva Lofton-Fitzsimmons, a Luiseño (La Jolla Band of Indians) woman from Southern California, traveled to Rome for Kateri's canonization in 2012. She journeyed to Vatican City with some of her family members and shared,

Figure 23 Lydia Johnson speaks about the Northwest Kateri Tekakwitha Spiritual Center. Credit: Michelle M. Jacob.

I think personally, and in our family, and in our church, our parish, always remembering Kateri and praying to her . . . has made her alive . . . and one of my nieces is named after her. And I think by the time I was going to the Tekakwitha conferences . . . I became more conscientious to do things on a continual basis . . . and Kateri was always a center of our whole fast [a spiritual tradition in the local mountains] and thinking and praying about Kateri's life, and trying to encourage us in our own life . . . and I've seen so many different people locally, and nation-wide, who would go to the conference faithfully every year, and I was encouraged by their faith. And I really appreciate during this pilgrimage, the words that were shared, everyone who spoke, because Kateri really did bring our people together in many ways . . . I think worldwide, you know, this Mohawk Lily, Kateri, the Lily of the Mohawks . . . you know, there was a time when the Church would look down on our tribal ceremonies, but I noticed now the priests will stay for our ceremonies . . . and the priests would stay for most of the ceremony, you know it's all night, but they would stay, and Father would say, "the more we pray for people the more we can help them." . . . I think the lessons of love one another and help one another, that's true in any faith. I think Kateri teaches us that and shows us that in her walk . . . I was so proud in the canonization for the pope to canonize her . . . to see it firsthand . . . it was very exciting.

Geneva shared that honoring her Indigenous cultural teachings and Catholic teachings was important in her own spiritual journey, and that Kateri serves as a powerful role model for her. She talked about how important it was that Kateri made it possible for the Church to formally recognize Native women as spiritual leaders:

> She was uniting us in so many ways . . . times are very difficult on the reservation . . . from health disparities to drugs and alcohol, there are so many issues our people have, and to have a patron saint is so special and important in so many ways. She's not only our saint, she's everybody's saint, but she's our Native saint . . . to see one of our people among those that are recognized . . . our spirituality will help keep our people strong . . . and Kateri will help encourage our people not to give up hope and be faithful, and I see Kateri as helping unite us and working towards what's spiritual and keep us strong . . . we need all the help we can get.

Geneva links the power of spirituality with the promise of addressing the challenges facing Indigenous communities today. She mentions health disparities and substance abuse as leading problems, and believes that the strong spiritual traditions of her people, along with Catholic traditions, will help provide a powerful way forward.

Sina Wi Gloria Chief Eagle-Carson, a Brule (Sicangu) Lakota woman who also attended Tekakwitha's canonization, had long hoped that she would witness Kateri's transformation into sainthood. Gloria first learned about Kateri Tekakwitha in a Kateri Circle in Salt Lake City. When I asked Gloria why Kateri was important, she replied,

> Because she is Indian . . . I say my prayers to her, and I would speak in Lakota. I would tell her, "you have to help me because you are also Indian and I'm Indian so you know what we're going through." And as a result she would answer my prayers almost instantly. And so I have great faith in her. And now that she is a saint she has even more power . . . I think that she is so powerful, even if you doubted her, just try her once . . . she's an intercessor. She intercedes for us. She asks God for whatever we ask for . . . that's how I believe. I also believe if you live your religion and think that way, you don't really have to ask for something . . . you'll get what you need . . . I like the Indian ways because they are so nice, aren't they? So humble. I never feel alone when I go to this [National Tekakwitha] conference, because we're all Native, and we're all Catholics . . . I love the lessons, the workshops they have.

Gloria finds community in the Tekakwitha Conference community, noting that she never feels alone there, and that she loves the cultural lessons in the workshops. She journeyed to Rome for the canonization in 2012, and is devoted to praying to Kateri for intercession. Gloria also combines Indigenous and Catholic traditions by praying to a Catholic saint, Kateri, in Lakota. Gloria notes that Kateri always answers her prayers.

Linda Azure (White Clay Nation) also made the pilgrimage to Kateri's canonization. She viewed the Indian Pilgrims as a powerful example of Indigenous community. Her mother was a true believer in Tekakwitha's power, attending the Tekakwitha Conferences, and "always praying to her, and for her." Linda wanted to attend the canonization on behalf of her mother and to honor the Indigenous saint. In our interview, Linda shared, "I really see what she believed in. And I don't think anybody outside of our culture really, really knows what it means to us . . . that she's a saint now. I don't think they understand that, what it really truly means to us and how much we've invested, how much we've walked with all our other cultures of our tribes,

with how much all our tribes have walked together for this one cause . . .
it's so powerful . . . we get it, you know, we understand each other."

Similarly, Alice Corbiere (Garden River First Nation Anishinaabe) stated
that she made the pilgrimage to Rome because "I was excited to see a First
Nation person canonized. I thought that would be a big honor." Alice said
she learned about Kateri "way back in grade school, sixty years ago or more,"
and prayed for her canonization throughout her life. In my interview with
her, Alice spoke about what Kateri's canonization meant to her:

> I was very impressed with the whole service . . . very impressed to see all the
> people wearing their different symbols of either their area, or their tribes, or
> their hometown areas. And then seeing the Aboriginal priests, nuns that was
> all was very, very impressive . . . and to see the whole world come together
> for a celebration. And the Catholic Church, it's got a lot of good points, but it
> also has some negative points, but it can certainly bring the world together in
> using the Mass. Everybody can participate . . . it was very impressive and very
> moving. Just talking about it is kind of making me a little emotional.

Alice mentions that she gets a "calming feeling" when she prays to Kateri,
who seems more personal than the other saints. Thus, Saint Kateri serves as
an important spiritual guide for Alice, who is "very impressed" with Kateri's
life, as she was a "strong woman and role model." Alice has worked in education and First Nations administration within her home community. She
shared that she felt a special commitment to encourage First Nations students to persevere in education. Alice also values upholding cultural traditions, noting that she brought special sacred items to wear at the canonization and that the Mass of Thanksgiving was especially meaningful to her,
as the Mass was a special celebration of Indigenous culture and language.
She sees this as a powerful example of countering "a lot of damage that took
place" through colonialism. In her home community, the tabernacle is made
of white birch bark, and she feels a special connection to the Church because
it demonstrates a respect for Indigenous culture, including through language and art in the celebration of Catholic Mass.

The examples in this section—from Mohawk women who care for the
community and the mission church in Akwesasne, to the Navajo/Diné

women who sew garments in Arizona and sell the blessed vestments at Indigenous gatherings, to Yakama women who adorn their mission church with Kateri decorations and use ancestral land to dedicate space for a Kateri center, to conference and canonization attendees who explain the importance of the Native woman saint—each demonstrate the ways in which Native women, perhaps the unlikeliest of agents within the Catholic Church, are indeed active in providing an alternative narrative about Kateri and Native peoples, compared to the master narratives that have dominated history. These Native women insist the logic of a dichotomous, either "traditional" or "Christian," understanding of Indigenous spiritual expression is flawed. The women are expressing the idea of "Indigenous principle" that Angela Tarango has analyzed; she articulates the "main idea behind the Indigenous principle is this: Christianity should be rooted in the culture of the missionized" (Tarango 2014, 5). Tarango argues that understanding "the Indigenous principle as practice also changes how scholars of American religion view Native American Christians . . . understanding it as a religious practice that became distinctly Indigenous (that is to say, Native American) allows us to see just one way that Native Americans have taken Christianity and have begun to dismantle its colonizing roots" (Tarango 2014, 175–76). We have seen how Mohawk, Navajo/Diné, Yakama, Lakota, Luiseño, Anishinaabe, and White Clay Nation women featured in this chapter draw from their traditional teachings to inform their actions, caring for their communities, protecting their cultural teachings, and representing their spiritual practices as Indigenous women devoted to Saint Kateri Tekakwitha. They recast land, bodies, and culture as sacred parts of their spiritual expression, placing Saint Kateri at the center of regenerative and supportive practices that affirm Indigenous arts, representation, language, culture, and land.

Conclusion: Reclaiming a Sacred Relationship with Mother Earth

The competing narratives that surround Saint Kateri help us understand the complexities of settler colonial logics and Indigenous peoples' resilient responses to them. While Indigenous peoples and homelands have been portrayed as dichotomously "heathen" or "virgin," one can see how the settler colonial imposed definitions and descriptions of Indigenous lands and bodies shift, sometimes radically so, to uphold the conquest of Indigenous lands. Within the Catholic master narratives, Tekakwitha is described as a beautiful, pure, virgin maiden, yet the violence and loss that surrounds her childhood, and the bloody, brutal, and ongoing violence she inflicted upon herself, is downplayed and recast as further evidence that Catholicism has saved her from her evil people and heathen family. As Darren Bonaparte (2009) writes, it is startling to discover Indigenous peoples "are the thorns" Kateri "transcends." Thus, Kateri is a figure around which there are multiple forms of unspeakable violence. The violence of settler colonialism and the violence of a young woman brutalizing her own body remain largely unspoken, hushed perhaps because speaking of the violence may call into question whether Catholicism really does bring peace and progress to Indigenous peoples. In contemporary times, Kateri becomes an idealized vision of Indigenous feminine beauty. Such an image helps Indigenous women to strengthen their spiritualities and engage in loving acts of community building. Kateri's followers portray her in multiple ways, spanning Indian Country. She is embraced as Indigenous kin; her followers insist "she listens to us" and "she is one of us." Kateri's brutal acts of self-harm remain unspeakable, perhaps because her followers fear young women will be too literal in looking up to Kateri as a role model. In that way, surely we do not want Indigenous girls "following in Kateri's footsteps."

The final form of unspeakable violence is the settler colonial logic that frames Indigenous peoples and homelands as inherently rapable. Indigenous bodies and lands are commodities to be counted, surveyed, assigned a value, and used for the pleasure of the settler colonial project. Indigenous agency is not valued, nor is an Indigenous perspective of land/environment, which honors "mutually reciprocal relations of giving and respectful treatment" (Langdon 2007, 263). Settler colonial logics remain largely unchanged within the structure of the nation-state, which holds so much power over Indigenous peoples. In Tekakwitha's time, the colonial powers fought and challenged Indigenous peoples, and each other, to lay down borders across Mohawk homeland, insisting each colonial power's "civilization" was supreme. Today, Mohawk peoples must carry settler-state identification to cross borders for employment, or to visit relatives who happen to live on the other side of a settler-state imposed border, whether Canadian or U.S. While historically, Kateri's body and land were praised as "virgin," today we see that the lust for Mohawk homeland and the natural resources it holds has led to the development of aluminum plants. Mohawk peoples continue to fight to protect their homelands, people, and cultural ways.

Part of this struggle is to define Saint Kateri from an Indigenous perspective. As Bonaparte argued, Tekakwitha was deeply valued and rooted in her culture, while many of the strengths the missionaries praised were due to her traditional cultural upbringing. Similarly, Mohawk peoples continue to fight to protect their homelands. The land is not, and never has been, for sale to the highest bidder; and Mohawk peoples resist the powers that be who seek to use and destroy Indigenous homeland. Corporate giants, the powerholders within contemporary settler-states, are being called to task by Mohawk peoples. Aluminum manufacturer Alcoa is now being held responsible for the damage they have done by poisoning the air, land, and water of Mohawk peoples. Even the U.S. government articulates, "two Alcoa plants in Massena, N.Y., discharged a stream of toxic pollutants into the water, air, and soil around them" (U.S. Department of Commerce 2013). As punishment, Alcoa is required to pay $19.4 million to atone for their damages to Mohawk peoples and homeland. The funding will help restore traditional culture practices, fisheries, and habitats. The children who attend the Akwesasne Freedom School will take part in some of these restoration activities. Mohawk women, who pray to Kateri and have been involved in the cultural revitalization work with Mohawk youth, are helping their people reclaim their traditions, bodies, and homelands. They are living in a way that honors their spiritual responsibility to Mother Earth. Their prayers and efforts help to reassert a Mohawk way of living and being, including caring for the land, which can inspire new "economic and policy forces that dominate human-environment relations" (Jenkins et al. 2006, 319). Next, in chapter 5, we will focus on specific ways that people can focus on transforming Western institutions into forces for radical social change that are necessary to decolonize our bodies, minds, and communities.

5
Conclusion

Join the Journey of Activism and Healing

Ethnographic Introduction: Water Walkers in San Diego

*T*he students buzzed around, washing produce, gathering art supplies, and delegating final tasks for their event, a Water Walk on the University of San Diego campus.

I watched them and resisted the urge to "tell them what to do." This is their event, and their good spirits permeate it. The Water Walk really represents the students' energy and intention with which they have infused the event—during their several weeks of planning, they have learned to communicate and collaborate with classmates with whom they probably wouldn't normally spend much time in direct communication. They worked collectively to plan the Water Walk, which would bring together members of the campus community, walking from the west end of campus to the middle of campus, stopping to discuss the importance of water at different points along the route.

The students asked me to say a few words at the beginning, and I agreed to explain how the Nibi Walks/Water Walks in the Great Lakes Region inspired the event. There, Anishinaabe women elders guide the gathering of people, collecting water, carrying it, and praying for the duration of the Water Walks.

Prayers are offered, encouraging humans to restore their sacred connections with water.

Later that day, I made my way to the designated starting point of the University of San Diego's first Water Walk. It was a cool spring day, with a breeze coming off of the Pacific Ocean. It looked like rain might begin—surely a blessing during California's devastating drought. A group of about twenty-five of us gathered at the Garden of the Sea, a lushly landscaped area that overlooks Mission Bay, San Diego Bay, and the Pacific Ocean. It is perhaps the most stunning view on our hillside campus. When the students decided it was time to start the event, I welcomed all the Water Walkers and explained that the students in my American Indian Health and Spirituality class had learned about Indigenous understandings of health and well-being, which teach that the health of the people is always connected to the health of the environment. We need to care for Mother Earth, as well as our own bodies. In my class, students learned about the Yu'pik concept of Ella, which reminds humans that our thoughts and actions have a deep impact on the environment. We are spiritually responsible for nurturing ourselves and the land, water, air, as well as all living beings. In the class, I also introduced students to the Nibi Walk/Water Walk events that were happening in the Great Lakes region. I told them about the National Tekakwitha Conference, where a woman presented about the experience of being on a Water Walk, traveling the entire length of the Mississippi River, from the headwaters in Anishinaabe homeland in the Great Lakes region, all the way to Indigenous homeland in the Gulf Coast region. In my class, we discussed the implications of people reclaiming their spiritual responsibilities to care for Mother Earth, to care for the water—recognizing it as a sacred gift from the Creator. The Water Walks are an expression of this concern. My students were inspired to host their own Water Walk out of respect for the tradition that Anishinaabe people and their allies had started. Our contact in Wisconsin sent us information about one of the 2015 Water Walks, and the students organized a San Diego walk in alliance—and to raise awareness among campus personnel about the sacredness of water.

The students debated what messages should be central in their Water Walk. They drafted and revised flyers. The final draft of the flyer was circulated on campus and sent, via our Tribal Liaison, to local tribal community members. The students wanted it to be an event that respected traditional tribal teach-

ings about caring for Mother Earth. The students also recognized their own responsibility to become educated about environmental-justice issues, and to help teach the Water Walk's attendees about the pressing need to do something about the California drought. The students had their own lenses through which they viewed the upcoming Water Walk, and they drew from their individual and collective perspectives to shape the messages they shared. They decided that one student should speak at each "stop" or "stage" of the Water Walk. They divided the labor. Some students chose to do research and create a handout that could educate attendees; others did research and prepared notecards to read from during the event—giving mini-presentations along the different stops of the Water Walk.

During the Water Walk, we stopped for a few minutes at each of several fountains on campus. At each fountain one student would read from his or her notecards, expressing some issue around water that was important to her or him. One student spoke about how the drought was impacting wildlife, including elk herds who were dying because their water sources in Northern California were drying up. Another student spoke about the increased risk of wildfires in California due to the extreme drought. Another student connected the drought and its dangers to climate change, urging us to think about ways that we contribute to climate change, and to recognize that Indigenous peoples and cultures bear a great burden in facing climate change. The students spoke from the heart. It was clear that this event helped them to develop a voice in support of these issues. It was a unique opportunity for them to create a venue to speak about these spiritual/intellectual issues outside of the classroom. They thrived under the conditions that they established for themselves—as Water Walkers. One student, who was unsure of what he could contribute to the event, ended up agreeing to be our Water Carrier. He used a beautiful handmade ceramic vessel to gather water from each of the fountains we visited during the Water Walk. It was clear that he understood how his contribution was important— he was carrying the sacred gift that inspired us all to participate in the event. He literally held in his hands the sacred gift from the Creator, which we were honoring that day. He held the precious resource, encouraging us all to reconnect in a spiritually responsible way. Our Water Walk gained attention as we traveled together around the campus. Several students and faculty members joined us en route, and we ended up with perhaps forty-five people.

Figure 24 Water Walkers at the University of San Diego in 2015. Credit: Ryan T. Blystone.

At the end of the Water Walk, several students had set up a gathering area with chalkboards, inviting people to use the chalk to express their artistic notions, thoughts, or feedback about the event, or about water in general. They had brought fresh fruit to share with all the Water Walkers. We delighted in the fresh watermelon, strawberries, and grapes. The students had also brought several succulent plants, and held a raffle to share these as gifts among the Water Walkers. They enjoyed sharing the gifts with the attendees and affirming everyone's presence. They smiled at one another, glad for the good spirit of the event. Later that afternoon it rained, and continued to rain, for two days. I thought back to our discussion of Ella and how the students' intentions may indeed have helped to quell the parched land of San Diego.

Healing and Activism: Starting Where You Are

The opening of this chapter shares a description of the Water Walk that my students organized at the University of San Diego (USD) campus. I follow the work of critical Indigenous studies scholars and feminist scholars who situate their writing and analyses within the concrete, lived experiences of their communities; in short, we begin our journeys of healing and activism by starting where we are. By doing so, we can develop everyday practices that "habituate us to take care of the world" (Lugones 2010, 742). Observation and lived experience fuel our knowledge of the world and ourselves, and inform our journeys of healing (Cajete 2000). Much of my work takes place within a university setting. In writing the ethnographic introduction to this chapter, I asked: How do the lessons I describe in *Indian Pilgrims* translate into concrete experiences in students' lives? This is one example of starting where we are, or as feminist scholar bell hooks writes, "When thinking of what to write I have always worked from the space of concrete experience, writing about what was happening in my life and the lives of females and males around me" (hooks 2015, ix). The students were inspired by the Nibi Walks, and decided to organize their own walk to show their respect and commitment to the principles outlined in Anishinaabe traditional teachings, which guide the Nibi Walks. The USD Water Walk was a small gathering, and it took place entirely on our small hilltop campus, with Water Walkers visiting several of our campus fountains. It was a small example of activism. Yet, for the students involved, and the other Water Walkers who participated, it was one of the first times that they experienced a collective of people on campus coming together to use our bodies, minds, and spirits to collectively engage with the idea of praying for water in a way that honored critical Indigenous studies, ethnic studies, and traditional Indigenous cultural teachings.

The last student to speak, a white male, shared that he was glad for the event, and glad for ethnic studies, because that was the place where students learn about Indigenous ways of viewing the world. The class was where he was exposed to Indigenous authors, which enriched his education and his own understanding of how his thoughts and actions matter in a broader collective sense of responsibility. It was an inspiring reflection of a university student "seeing" how he matters. That is one of the main messages of *Indian Pilgrims*. We all matter. All of our efforts toward healing and activism matter.

This conclusion chapter has the intention of helping readers focus on the main points throughout the book. We will briefly review the primary lessons shared in each chapter; then we will reach out a bit further to apply what we have learned in *Indian Pilgrims*. This chapter concludes by helping readers think about how other Western institutions could be changed to better fit the needs of Native peoples, and by extension, all peoples who want lives that are rooted in a sense of collectivism, which helps encourage and inspire us to reach toward activism and healing.

Lessons of Spiritual Responsibility

In chapter 1, we were introduced to the holy woman, Kateri Tekakwitha, who is credited with intervening to help answer peoples' prayers. Major lessons from the book demonstrate how Saint Kateri's devotees inspire Indigenous-led movements to create a space that honors the Native feminine as spiritually powerful. The primary components of this movement-building work are: drawing on traditions to build strong communities, caring for one another, strengthening the spiritual power and presence of one another, and ultimately healing oneself, one's community, and Mother Earth. bell hooks uses a feminist analysis to encourage us to link our spirituality with a vision for social justice; she writes, "restoring our respect for the sacred feminine, it has helped us find ways to affirm and/or reaffirm the importance of spiritual life. Identifying liberation from any form of domination and oppression as essentially a spiritual quest returns us to a spirituality, which unites spiritual practice with our struggles for justice and liberation. A feminist vision of spiritual fulfillment is naturally the foundation of authentic spiritual life" (hooks 2015, 109). All peoples, communities, and lands need healing. These powerful lessons can be shared to heal a greater collective.

In chapter 2, readers learned about the concept of Indigenous environmentalism and its four main components: 1) Spiritual Responsibility; 2) Listening to Tribal Elders; 3) Looking Downstream and Looking Upstream; and 4) Embracing Allies Who Understand the Shared Responsibility of Protecting Mother Earth. We examined the principles of Indigenous environmentalism as illustrated with an image of Tahoma, the beautiful and sacred mountain who watches over the city of Seattle, and oversaw Jake Finkbonner's miraculous healing that served as the clinching miracle to propel Kateri

Tekakwitha into official Catholic sainthood. Tahoma helps us recognize the sacred land that has fostered cultural teachings, which inform Indigenous environmentalism. The concept of Indigenous environmentalism affirms our spiritual responsibility to care for Mother Earth. We explored several ways in which Kateri Tekakwitha inspires activism to rethink our relationship with the environment. Water Walkers, who are growing in numbers and influence, shared some of their ideas at the National Tekakwitha Conference in Fargo, North Dakota, an area of booming economic development, which is tied to the resource extraction of oil and gas through fracking. While there are benefits to the economic growth that we are seeing in areas being fracked, the long-term implications are not as optimistic. Fracking produces wastewater that is laced with toxic chemicals, many of which are not tested or monitored due to industry secrets forbidding people from knowing the exposure to harmful chemicals to which they, their children, pets, and food have been subjected. When one applies an intergenerational lens to this form of economic development,—as in the case of asking, how will this resource extraction benefit the next seven generations?—one can see how the extraction and burning of oil will likely do more harm to future generations, with very little benefit. Mother Earth is scarred in the process, and our water, air, and land is contaminated, while energy corporations insist that we cannot "prove" they are liable. The court system, with its burden of proof shaded to benefit the corporations, will likely offer no solutions that will benefit future generations either.

When my students and I pour over the evidence of the short-term benefits of economic and energy development systems that are mainstream in the United States and Canada, students often become upset and sad about the lack of respect for Mother Earth. They wonder why we do not place a greater value on Indigenous knowledge systems, which urge us to use an intergenerational lens. Through application of Indigenous knowledge, however, students quickly learn that they themselves have a responsibility to work for their own transformation, for their communities, and the policies that shape our society. There is a place for them to contribute to social change rooted in Native feminism; they, too, can participate in dreaming for a better future for our people (Hilden and Lee 2010). Their thoughts, intentions, and actions have an impact—and as discussed in chapter 3, the students are implicated in all matters of community building. The principles of community building, illustrated on the back of a turtle, apply to each and every one of us, and this is a lesson that the students embraced when they decided to organize a Water Walk on campus. Along with their education, students have access to resources, and they have the possibility of advocating for radical social change. When we examine the implications of climate change and our shortsighted energy and economic development approaches, students know that they are accountable to Mother Earth and the future generations. They accept their spiritual responsibility to live differently, to share information, to have discussions with their peers and families. They resolve to build community around these issues, and to change the way that humans relate to the environment—they will rethink their actions, our policies, and our systems through lenses that are respectful of Indigenous cultural teachings (Bahr 2015).

Honoring traditional teachings that uphold collectivist ideals means that we also need to recognize that every being is sacred. My students, while grappling with the application of Indigenous cultural teachings, embody this lesson. Indigenous studies classes bring a diverse set of students together. None of my students who organized the USD Water Walk identified as Indigenous, yet some had taken several ethnic studies classes and were superstars within the major, had already mastered advanced theories, and had a broad knowledge of the literature. For students of color who are ethnic studies majors, they can see how Native feminist analyses serve their home communities. White students in our major critically analyze racism and social injustices from their identities as allies who work to break patterns of inequality as they rethink the history and their relationship to Indigenous homeland (Tuck and Yang 2012). Other students, however, are new to ethnic studies. These students, sometimes coming from wealthy white suburbs, are just beginning to learn about race, colonization, and social inequalities. It makes for an interesting sixteen weeks together. I see the students grow together. They begin to find ways to build community. The privileged white male who is taking the ethnic studies class in his last semester as a senior, "because he needs a 'diversity' class to graduate," became our Water Carrier during the Water Walk. He stepped into the role of responsibility and later gave a presentation about how that experience helped him to see that he has a valuable contribution to make in a collective effort for social change—to build a collective that is founded upon the ideal that we are all sacred; we all need to restore our spiritual responsibility to Mother Earth; and we all benefit from being on the challenging path toward decolonization. When we find ways to discuss and implement forms of collectivist thinking, we are building community in powerful ways, affirming that everyone has something valuable to offer. This vision of inclusivity is at the heart of feminism.

In my work to examine the meaning and importance of a historical figure, Kateri Tekakwitha, I follow Myla Vicenti Carpio's example of situating my work in American Indian studies by centering "sovereignty and Indigenousness itself" to produce scholarship that articulates the wisdom of Indigenous cultural teachings, to propose ways forward that address persistent problems facing our communities, and to engage how the past informs the present (Vicenti Carpio 2011, xxiv). In chapter 3, we examined principles of community building and analyzed community building in diverse settings across the Yakama Reservation in the Pacific Northwest, the Water Walks in the Great Lakes region, the work of Sister Clissene in the Southwest, and the persistence of Indigenous culture on the Louisiana Bayou. We also engaged with men's devotion to Saint Kateri as a powerful pathway toward community building, with visionary examples from Deacon Sid and Ray Williams, as well as among non-Native men and clergy. Within each of these examples, we saw Indigenous peoples and allies upholding the principles of community building: 1) Interconnecting—Our physical health is connected to the spiritual well-being of our people; 2) Honoring—We must work toward a way of life that honors and celebrates the contributions that all people make; 3) Embracing Responsibility—We all have a role to play in building a healthy community; and 4) Instructing—Our cultural traditions are sacred instructions given to us by the Creator. Across diverse identities and settings, Indigenous peoples are upholding these principles, which are shared within traditional cultural teachings.

Myla Vicenti Carpio (2011) provides an excellent analysis of the complexities of Indigenous identity, noting that simplistic dichotomies mask the nuances of people's lives. In her work, she explains that although the dichotomy of "urban" versus "reservation" Indian is commonly used, Indigenous peoples themselves resist this simple dichotomy, with many people living with an urban address maintaining strong ties to their reservations and "engag[ing] in a pattern of constant movement between the reservation and the city" (Vicenti Carpio 2011, xxiii). She provides a useful framework for me to build upon as I seek to examine the importance of Indigenous Catholicism.

Too often Indigenous peoples, for a variety of reasons, have been pushed into the binary of "Indian" or "Catholic." Part of the reason why Saint Kateri Tekakwitha is so popular among Indigenous peoples (Catholic and non-Catholic alike) is that she, as a symbol, embodies the breaking of constraining dichotomies. While Indigenous peoples have different relationships with Christianity and the man-made Christian institutions that are so prevalent on our reservations, we must acknowledge that Indigenous Catholicism is indeed an important part of many of our communities. Sister Archambault, who embraced both her Indigenous/Lakota traditions and Catholic traditions, reflects, "In maturing, I've learned that the truth, for me, lies in the union of the Lakota ways and the Catholic faith. In our modern world, often we find truth by passing through profound spiritual, social, cultural and economic displacement. I write from that uncomfortable place, where millions of the globe's inhabitants are thrust now, with no secure home, no freedom to live according to their cultural heritage" (Archambault 1998, 38). Many of our community members remember the violence of colonialism and conquest that often brought Christianity to our home communities, and we must also remember that the telling of histories from Indigenous peoples' perspectives, in all our diversity, is needed. Historian Jeffrey Shepherd articulates the stakes of critical Indigenous histories and identifies such work as an important part of decolonization. Shepherd instructs us, "Decolonization points to the struggles of Indigenous peoples to reclaim lands, traditions, and a sense of collective purpose. It seeks a place of healing from historical trauma and violence, while at the same time carving a space for indigeneity in the modern world. . . . Decolonization requires the awareness of the origins of conquest, the implications of exploitation, resistance to that oppression, and a recovery of traditions and memories that define Indigenous identity" (Shepherd 2010, 9–10). Shepherd reminds us that it is important to place Indigenous voices and perspectives at the center of decolonizing analyses because "Native people, rather than savages or victims, are complex historical actors who shape their own histories and have unique perspectives on the past" (Shepherd 2010, 10).

Similarly, Myla Vicenti Carpio reminds us, "As historians, educators, or makers of historical memory, we must question and become aware of whose narratives we privilege" (Vicenti Carpio 2011, 128). Any efforts toward decolonization must address the history of and narratives about Indigenous homeland. Hualapai leader Wilfred Whatoname Sr. explains: "History tells us of how the colonists and pilgrims immigrated from Europe and settled in the eastern part of the continent, and how they trekked out to the western part of the country. However, it does not always explain in detail how lands were taken, and how the Indians were eventually removed from lands they had inhabited from time immemorial" (Whatoname 2010, xiii). Part of our collective healing journey requires that we link the damages of history with the problems of today, as we examined in chapter 4, in the terms used by feminist scholars, "painful dismembering of families and societies" and the "unspeakable violence" of colonialism, and draw from the strengths of Indigenous cultural teachings to articulate a pathway forward of activism and healing. We saw how Indigenous women from diverse communities across Turtle Island carry on traditions of praying to Saint Kateri and thus are reclaiming a vision of the Native feminine as sacred.

The final main lesson of *Indian Pilgrims*, featured most prominently in chapter 4, is that Native feminist analyses offers us a helpful path forward as we disrupt colonial logics and reclaim Indigenous cultural and spiritual teachings. When we reclaim the Native feminine as sacred, we actively work toward gender justice, which was defined in chapter 1. Gender justice is a process of respecting the autonomy of women and encouraging collectivist thinking and strategizing, while working toward collective remedies that challenge the colonial and capitalist status quo (Smith 2008, 161). Working toward gender justice is a powerful form of decolonization, which has benefits for Indigenous communities and Western institutions alike. When we think about the gender justice problems in so many settings—whether it is domestic violence, sexual violence, poverty, wage gaps, child abuse, or murder—we all suffer as a result of these forms of physical, institutional, and structural violence. These shared problems require a collectivist approach. We also need to break the colonial logics that continue to perpetuate sexism and racism throughout society; we all need to heal from the Cycle of Destruction, which holds all of us back. As discussed in chapter 1, we need to shift from a Cycle of Destruction to a Cycle of Healing; the lessons outlined in *Indian Pilgrims* offer us a pathway forward as we learn about the devastating effects of colonial logics that have damaged all peoples. When we resist colonial logics, all peoples embark on a path of healing. We see many inspirational examples of healing all around us. *Indian Pilgrims* shares several examples of Native women who practice Native feminism in their everyday lived experiences. They gently, committedly walk the path of caring for the land, their communities, and their own spiritual well-being. They look to Saint Kateri Tekakwitha to inspire them and sustain them in their efforts. May we all find that path of inspiration and commitment to activism and healing.

Throughout *Indian Pilgrims*, we have seen how important the Native-led nonprofit organization National Tekakwitha Conference has been in providing many examples of healing through the inspiration of Saint Kateri Tekakwitha. The National Tekakwitha Conference brings together diverse peoples who all love and care for their communities across Turtle Island. In *Indian Pilgrims*, we have learned about Navajo/Diné elders Vi and Hazel, who were inspired by their Indigenous Blessing Way ceremony and worked together to sew and minister in honor of Saint Kateri. We also discussed the important work being accomplished by the Water Walkers, who pray for the health of the Mississippi River and all water and Indigenous homeland. We also discussed strong Native women who have chosen to enter into religious life, such as Sister Kateri Mitchell, Sister Archambault, and Sister Clissene Lewis, who have an unwavering commitment to respect and care for Indigenous communities. My research for *Indian Pilgrims*, guided by my attendance at the National Tekakwitha Conference and my own network of tribal peoples, has provided us with many examples of what it means to be on a path of resisting colonial logics and to work toward healing. Sister Kateri Mitchell, Mohawk Turtle Clan member and executive director of the National Tekakwitha Conference, serves as a powerful role model and inspiration to the National Tekakwitha Conference members; she leads the national organization, which has hosted an annual gathering for the past seventy-six years. When she was reflecting on the meaning and importance of Kateri Tekakwitha's (then) upcoming canonization, Sister Kateri wrote in a letter to her organization's members and linked Saint Kateri's sainthood with greater representation and voice of Indigenous peoples. Sister Kateri Mitchell wrote, "What glorious recognition and affirmation for the once invisible and voiceless First Peoples of Turtle Island! What a wonderful celebration for the hundreds who will travel to the Vatican, the Eternal City. Our Kateri Tekakwitha, a young Mohawk/Algonquin has brought many to a deeper faith, prayer life through healing and hope for her people" (Mitchell 2012, 130). Thus, Saint Kateri is important as a symbol of peace and healing. She symbolizes the rising of Indigenous peoples above the wounds of colonialism. Her sainthood symbolizes visibility and voice of Indigenous peoples upon Indigenous homeland and transnationally. Her sainthood represents and inspires a new/old understanding of the inherent goodness, worthiness, and beauty of Indigenous peoples and cultures.

Indigenous Catholicism: Indigenous Cultural Gifts

Chad Hamill, a Spokan scholar, writes about the importance of Indigenous cultures within Catholicism (Hamill 2012). He articulates that Indigenous cultural traditions emphasize that having a relationship with the spiritual world is a sign of well-being. Hamill's work documents the ways in which tribal peoples use song to make a connection to the spiritual world. The Mohawk women I interviewed at Akwesasne agreed that song is a powerful way to access the spiritual world. Their efforts to revitalize Mohawk language through the Akwesasne Freedom School and the Mohawk hymns sung in their Indigenous language are testament to the ways that an Indigenous Catholicism can help people on a path toward healing by reclaiming culture and language. The Akwesasne Freedom School, an immersion school for kindergarten through eighth-grade education, is a strong example of resisting colonial logics. On the school's website, which is designed to communicate the importance of the school's mission to English language visitors, one can view the Thanksgiving Address/Prayer: Ohenton Kariwahtekwen (Akwesasne Freedom School 2012). The Thanksgiving address gives thanks to the Creator for people, Mother Earth, water, fish, plants, food plants, medicine herbs, animals, trees, birds, four winds, thunder, sun,

Grandmother Moon, stars, teachers, and the Creator. It is a beautiful prayer that reminds us of the centrality of the natural world in Indigenous cultures and spirituality. In the section that honors Mother Earth, it reads, "We are all thankful to our Mother, the Earth, for she gives us all that we need for life. She supports our feet as we walk about upon her. It gives us joy that she continues to care for us as she has from the beginning of time. To our mother, we send greetings and thanks. Now our minds are one" (Akwesasne Freedom School 2012). The section that honors the Creator reads, "Now we turn our thoughts to the creator, or Great Spirit, and send greetings and thanks for all the gifts of creation. Everything we need to live a good life is here on this Mother Earth. For all the love that is still around us, we gather our minds together as one and send our choicest words of greetings and thanks to the Creator. Now our minds are one" (Akwesasne Freedom School 2012). The attention to honoring the Earth, all of creation, and the Creator's gifts to the people are central themes in Indigenous spiritualties.

Caring for Mother Earth

One of the greatest contributions Indigenous cultures can make to Catholicism is the reminder of the need to care for Mother Earth. Chapter 2 detailed examples of Indigenous people's struggles to protect Indigenous homeland from the shortsighted greed of capitalist neoliberal development. In the "New Indian Wars," Indigenous peoples are fighting settler nation-states and multinational corporations for the right to protect the water, air, and land from environmental destruction (Silko 1981). Saint Kateri Tekakwitha, the Patroness of the Environment, can perhaps inspire a greater effort on behalf of Catholics and the Church to enter into activism to care for Mother Earth. Perhaps Catholics will be inspired to become more educated and politically involved in environmental struggles all over Turtle Island and beyond.

For example, will Catholics take a greater stand against energy policies that we know are polluting our bodies and Mother Earth, such as the dependence on coal, a nineteenth-century technology? We see the effects of reliance on coal, and the policies that encourage coal energy dependence. The widespread use of coal as a supposedly "cheap" form of energy, in fact, has significant negative impacts, compromising our environmental health, air, and water. Coal is a risky backbone to our energy system (Porter 2014). In chapter 2, we considered the nexus of cultural identity, race, and environment in our analysis of environmental problems across Turtle Island and drew from Jeffrey Shepherd's argument that decolonization is needed in resisting neocolonial politics and development (Shepherd 2010, 189). We can celebrate Yakama peoples' resistance to the coal terminals that would destroy sacred salmon fisheries.

In 2015, Duke Energy, the largest electrical utility in the United States, was found guilty in federal court for "polluting four major rivers for several years with toxic coal ash from five power plants in North Carolina" (Zucchino 2015). One of the reasons that coal, as a source of electricity, is problematic is because after it is burned, the coal ash needs to be stored somewhere. Typically, utilities store the coal ash in unlined pits next to waterways. And, as it has been documented, "Coal ash slurry contains toxic heavy metals including arsenic, lead and mercury, which can contaminate groundwater, streams and rivers while also polluting the air" (ibid.) Duke Energy has acknowledged it has at least two hundred seeps of coal ash in North Carolina alone, with plants releasing 3 million gallons of coal ash water a day (ibid.).

In addition to the need to wean ourselves from the addiction to seemingly cheap electricity through burning coal, we also need to rethink our addiction to oil. The United States seems to have an insatiable appetite for oil. Hydraulic fracturing or "fracking" is a growing economic enterprise on Turtle Island. Again, we see how the settler colonial nation-state works hand in hand with multinational energy companies to slant policy and regulation to promote the development of fracking. In *Indian Pilgrims* we have examined this issue in terms of the sandstone mining in the Great Lakes region, as well as the oil industry-caused erosion in the bayou. In California, where fracking is most prevalent in Kern Country, the lack of regulation and oversight is leaving many people wondering about the risks of drinking-water contamination (Lifsher 2015). One of the problems with fracking is that it relies on a mix of water, sand, and chemicals to be injected into the ground to release the natural gas and oil stored in Mother Earth. The wastewater from this process, laced with chemicals of unknown source and quantity (due to "industry secret" legal protections, which allow oil companies to hide the names and quantities of chemicals used in their fracking operations), then must be stored—in wells dug for waste disposal near the drilling sites. California is struggling with drought conditions, and while the public is wringing its hands over the need to remove lawns and take shorter showers, in the San Joaquin Valley, oil companies are using precious water to create a chemical cocktail to be used for fracking, then putting the contaminated water back into Mother Earth as a "waste" that cannot be treated.

Perhaps Saint Kateri Tekakwitha can inspire us to rethink our energy consumption, to become educated about the sources of our energy, and to advocate for policies guided by Indigenous environmentalism, which take into account the true costs of the ways in which we currently supply our energy markets. Perhaps we can draw from Indigenous cultural teachings, develop a stronger relationship with the spiritual world, and collectively envision a spiritual revolution for our energy economy. We are all in need of a healing path forward (Tinker 2014). See appendix 2, "You Can Join the Journey of Activism and Healing," to consider ways we might move forward on such a journey.

Where Will Your Journey Take You?

I invite readers to read through the discussion questions in appendix 1. The questions, which USD Water Walk students helped to revise, are designed to encourage readers to engage the main points of *Indian Pilgrims*, think about how the lessons apply to one's own life, and connect the lessons in *Indian Pilgrims* within one's local context. In this way, readers are invited to become storytellers in their own right. We all have insights that can be used to extend the concept of Indigenous environmentalism; to articulate how Saint Kateri Tekakwitha might inspire another generation's spirituality, community building, and care for Mother Earth; and to collectively work toward gender justice.

Appendix 1
Discussion Questions

Indian Pilgrims: Indigenous Journeys of Activism and Healing with Saint Kateri Tekakwitha

Please use these questions to encourage further thoughts and actions about the main lessons in *Indian Pilgrims*. I invite you to use the questions as an individual reader, with your family and friends to encourage discussions, within reading groups or community meetings, in the classroom, or at your workplace. Everyone has good ideas to contribute about the environment, building community, and spirituality!

1. Who are some of the diverse peoples who honor Saint Kateri?
2. Describe at least two different interpretations of Saint Kateri's importance. For example, do some of Saint Kateri's devotees focus more on her Catholic identity, Mohawk identity, Indigenous identity, female identity, or some combination?
3. How is Saint Kateri an important Native feminine spiritual figure?
4. What is gender justice? For whom does gender justice matter? Who benefits from gender justice?

5. How does Indigenous environmentalism differ from other forms of environmentalism you have heard about or practiced?

6. Catholicism is a religion that was brought to Indigenous people along with colonization. Is the idea of an Indigenous Catholicism an unresolvable contradiction? Why or why not?

7. Who is one of your favorite people you read about in *Indian Pilgrims*? Why?

8. What is one of your favorite photos or images in *Indian Pilgrims*? Why?

9. What is one of the most important social issues or problems you read about in *Indian Pilgrims*? Why?

10. Describe the principles of community building articulated in *Indian Pilgrims*. Which of these principles resonates with you? How might you engage in deeper levels of community building?

11. Who are the people Indigenous to the land where you go to school, attend church, work, or live? Do they have ideas that can inform our understanding of Indigenous environmentalism? What are the environmental/spiritual issues that concern them? How can you support Indigenous grassroots activism at the local level?

Appendix 2
You Can Join the Journey of Activism and Healing

W hat can you do to join the journey of activism and healing that *Indian Pilgrims* advocates? Listed below is a set of ideas to help you brainstorm the path of your journey. Reflect on these ideas and share them, and/or create a list of your own ideas. Perhaps you can share some of these ideas, which may encourage broader discussion and movement toward healing, with your friends, family, church members, neighbors, communities, coworkers, and social media contacts.

1. Find out where the sources of your energy supply are. For example, does your home or office depend on coal, oil, natural gas, nuclear, or hydroelectric power? Do you use solar or wind power? Where are the land bases from which your power sources originate? Who are the Indigenous peoples in these locations?

2. If you are inspired by the activities of attendees at the National Tekakwitha Conference, consider attending a national or regional conference. Helpful sources are:

National Tekakwitha Conference: www.tekconf.org
Tekakwitha Conference Archives at Marquette University: http://www
.marquette.edu/library/archives/Mss/TC/TC-sc.shtml
Kateri Northwest Ministry Institute: http://katerinmi.org/index.html

3. If you are drawn to the concept of Indigenous environmentalism, these
   excellent organizations will be great resources for you:

Indigenous Environmental Network: http://www.ienearth.org/
Native Communities and Climate Change Project: http://www.tribes
andclimatechange.org/index.php
Honor the Earth: http://www.honorearth.org/
Great Lakes Indian Fish and Wildlife Commission: http://www.glifwc
.org/index.html

Appendix 3
Interview Guide

1. How did you learn about Kateri?
2. Why is Kateri important to you?
3. How long have you been honoring Kateri? Do you have a favorite memory or activity from this time? How has Kateri helped you? Or others you know?
4. Tell me one of your favorite stories about Kateri.
5. How is Kateri important for American Indian culture? Does she help you combine Indigenous and Catholic traditions?
6. What message about Kateri do you have for future generations?
7. Optional: Would you like me to take a photograph of you or one of your belongings (e.g., regalia, keepsake) to help show the importance of Kateri in your life?

Bibliography

Ackerman, Lillian A. 2000. "Complementary but Equal: Gender Status in the Plateau." In *Women and Power in Native North America*, edited by Laura F. Klein and Lillian A. Ackerman. Norman: University of Oklahoma Press.

Akwesasne Freedom School. 2012. "Akwesasne Freedom School." Accessed May 23, 2015. http://www.freedom-school.org/index.php/thanksgiving.

Akwesasne Mohawk Wake Choir. 2006. "TEION KWARI WAKON: Selections of Mohawk Hymns." Akwesasne Mohawk Wake Choir.

Alfred, Gerald R. 1995. *Heeding the Voices of our Ancestors: Kahnawake Mohawk Politics and the Rise of Native Nationalism*. Toronto: Oxford University Press.

Alfred, Taiaiake. 2005. *Wasáse: Indigenous Pathways of Action and Freedom*. Peterborough, Ontario: Broadview Press.

Archambault, Marie Therese. 1998. *A Retreat with Black Elk: Living in the Sacred Hoop*. Cincinnati: St. Anthony Messenger Press.

Arvin, Maile, Eve Tuck, and Angie Morrill. 2013. "Decolonizing Feminism: Challenging Connections between Settler Colonialism and Heteropatriarchy." *Feminist Formations* 25 (1 Spring): 8–34.

Associated Press. 2015. "Mining Company Closing Office in Northern Wisconsin." Green Bay Press Gazette. Accessed November 13, 2015. http://www.greenbaypress gazette.com/story/news/local/2015/02/27/mining-company-closing-office-in-northern -wisconsin/24143529/.

Bahr, Ann Marie B. 2015. "People of Place, Ehics of Earth: Indigenous Nations, Inter-faith Dialogue, and Environmental Sustainability." *Journal of Ecumenical Studies* 50 (1): 66–76.

Barber, Katrine. 2005. *Death of Celilo Falls*. Seattle: University of Washington Press.

Benedictine Sisters of Perpetual Adoration. 2014. "Sister professes vows in preparation of new Native American community." Last Modified January 13, 2014. Accessed September 16, 2014. http://www.benedictinesisters.org/articledetail.php?id=275&start=0&status=1&m_year=2014.

Bomberry, Victoria. 2012. "Indigenous Autonomy in Twenty-First-Century Bolivia." In *Comparative Indigeneities of the Américas: Toward a Hemispheric Approach*, edited by María Bianet Castellanos, Lourdes Gutiérrez Nájera, and Arturo J. Aldama, 213–26. Tucson: University of Arizona Press.

Bonaparte, Darren. 2009. *A Lily Among Thorns: The Mohawk Repatriation of Kateri Tekahkwitha*. Ahkwesahsne Mohawk Territory: The Wampum Chronicles.

Brayboy, B. M., and D. Deyhle. 2000. "Insider-Outsider: Researchers in American Indian Communities." *Theory into Practice* 39 (3): 163–69.

Bureau of Catholic Indian Missions. 2013. "Saint Kateri Tekakwitha: A Pilgrimage into Her Heart." Washington, DC: Bureau of Catholic Indian Missions.

Cajete, Gregory A. 2000. *Native Science: Natural Laws of Interdependence*. Santa Fe, NM: Clear Light Publishers.

Casey, Jack. 2012. *Kateri: Lily of the Mohawks*. Albany, NY: Staff Picks Press.

Centers for Disease Control and Prevention. 2014. "American Indian and Alaska Native death rates nearly 50 percent greater than those of non-Hispanic whites." Last Modified April 22, 2014. Accessed December 8, 2014. http://www.cdc.gov/media/releases/2014/p0422-natamerican-deathrate.html.

Chang, David A. 2011. "Enclosures of Land and Sovereignty." *Radical History Review* (109): 108–19. doi: 10.1215/01636545-2010-18.

Child, Brenda J., and Brian Klopotek, eds. 2014. *Indian Subjects: Hemispheric Perspectives on the History of Indigenous Education*. Santa Fe, NM: School for Advanced Research Press.

Clairmont, Kathryn. 2012. "Kathryn Clairmont Oral History Transcript." In *Native Footsteps: Along the Path of Saint Kateri Tekakwitha*, edited by Mark G. Thiel and Christopher Vecsey, 145–47. Milwaukee, WI: Marquette University Press.

Collins, Patricia Hill. 1998. *Fighting Words*. Minneapolis: University of Minnesota Press.

Collins, Patricia Hill. 2000. *Black Feminist Thought*. New York: Routledge.

Colombi, Benedict J. 2012. "Salmon and the Adaptive Capacity of Nimiipuu (Nez Perce) Culture to Cope with Change." *American Indian Quarterly* 36 (1): 75–97.

Costo, Rupert, and Jeannette Henry Costo, eds. 1987. *The Missions of California: A Legacy of Genocide*. San Francisco: Indian Historian Press.

Coté, Charlotte. 2010. *Spirits of Our Whaling Ancestors: Revitalizing Makah and Nuu-chah-nulth Traditions*. Seattle; Vancouver: University of Washington Press; University of British Columbia Press.

Coulthard, Glen Sean. 2014. *Red Skin, White Masks: Rejecting the Colonial Politics of Recognition*. Minneapolis: University of Minnesota Press.

Crawford O'Brien, Suzanne J. 2013. *Coming Full Circle: Spirituality and Wellness Among Native Communities in the Pacific Northwest*. Lincoln: University of Nebraska Press.

da Silva, Denise Ferreira. 2007. *Toward a Global Idea of Race*. Minneapolis: University of Minnesota Press.

Davenport, Coral. 2015. "Citing Climate Change, Obama Rejects Construction of Keystone XL Oil Pipeline." *New York Times*. Accessed November 10, 2015.

Deloria, Philip. 1998. *Playing Indian*. New Haven, CT: Yale University Press.

Deloria, Vine. 2003. *God Is Red: A Native View of Religion*. Golden, CO: Fulcrum Publishing.

Deloria, Vine, Jr. 1992. *God Is Red*. 2nd ed. Golden, CO: North American Press.

———. 2006. "Indian Affairs: Hebrews 13:8." In *Eating Fire, Tasting Blood*, edited by Marijo Moore, 52–62. New York: Thunder's Mouth Press.

Driskill, Quo-Li, Chris Finley, Brian Joseph Gilley, and Scott Lauria Morgensen, eds. 2011. *Queer Indigenous Studies: Critical Interventions in Theory, Politics, and Literature*.

Duran, Eduardo. 2006. *Healing the Soul Wound: Counseling with American Indians and Other Native Peoples*. New York: Teachers College Press.

Duran, Eduardo, and Bonnie Duran. 1995. *Native American Postcolonial Psychology*. Albany: State University of New York Press.

Earth Resource Foundation. 2014. "Polystyrene Foam Report." Accessed September 15, 2014. http://www.earthresource.org/campaigns/capp/capp-styrofoam.html.

Elder, Susan Blanchard. 1912. Adrien Rouquette. In *The Catholic Encyclopedia*. New York: Robert Appleton Company.

Fienup-Riordan, Ann, and Alice Rearden. 2012. *Ellavut, Our Yup'ik World and Weather: Continuity and Change on the Bering Sea Coast*. Seattle; Anchorage, AK: University of Washington Press; Calista Elders Council.

Fraga, Brian. 2014. "'Feminized' Church comment sparks debate Catholic leaders react to Cardinal Burke's interview regarding the 'man crisis' and the role of women." *Our Sunday Visitor Newsweekly.* Accessed February 2, 2015. https://www .osv.com/osvnewsweekly/article/tabid/535/artmid/13567/articleid/16784/%E2 %80%98feminized%E2%80%99-church-comment-sparks-debate.aspx?ref=top10.

Fur, Gunlog. 2002. "'Some Women Are Wiser Than Some Men': Gender and Native American History." In *Clearing a Path*, edited by Nancy Shoemaker, 75–103. New York: Routledge.

Garrett, J. T., and Michael Walkingstick Garrett. 1994. "The Path of Good Medicine: Understanding and Counseling Native American Indians." *Journal of Multicultural Counseling and Development* 22 (3): 134–44.

Gone, J. P. 2009. "A Community-Based Treatment for Native American Historical Trauma: Prospects for Evidence-Based Practice." *Journal of Consulting and Clinical Psychology* 77 (4): 751–62. doi: 10.1037/a0015390.

———. 2010. "Psychotherapy and Traditional Healing for American Indians: Exploring the Prospects for Therapeutic Integration." *The Counseling Psychologist* 38 (2): 166–235. doi: 10.1177/0011000008330831.

Gonzales, Sandra M. 2012. "Colonial Borders, Native Fences." In *Comparative Indigeneities of the Américas: Toward a Hemispheric Approach*, edited by María Bianet Castellanos, Lourdes Gutiérrez Nájera, and Arturo J. Aldama, 307–20. Tucson: University of Arizona Press.

Good Stiker, Duane. 1996. "TEK Wars: First Nations' Struggles for Environmental Planning." In *Defending Mother Earth: Native American Perspectives on Environmental Justice*, edited by Jace Weaver, 144–52. Maryknoll, NY: Orbis Books.

Gray, Mark, Mary Gautier, and Thomas S. J. Gaunt. 2014. "Cultural Diversity in the Catholic Church in the United States." Center for Applied Research in the Apostolate at Georgetown University.

Green, Rayna. 1988. "The Tribe Called Wannabee: Playing Indian in America and Europe." *Folklore* 99 (1): 30–55.

Greer, Allan. 2005. *Mohawk Saint.* New York: Oxford University Press.

Guidotti-Hernández, Nicole Marie. 2011. *Unspeakable Violence: Remapping U.S. and Mexican National Imaginaries.* Durham, NC: Duke University Press.

Gutiérrez Nájera, Lourdes, María Bianet Castellanos, and Arturo J. Aldama. 2012. Introduction. In *Comparative Indigeneities of the Américas: Toward a Hemispheric*

Approach, edited by María Bianet Castellanos, Lourdes Gutiérrez Nájera, and Arturo J. Aldama, 1–19. Tucson: University of Arizona Press.

Hamill, Chad. 2012. *Songs of Power and Prayer in the Columbia Plateau: The Jesuit, the Medicine Man, and the Indian Hymn Singer*. Corvallis: Oregon State University Press.

Helfrich, Joel T. 2014. "Cultural Survival in Action: Ola Cassadore Davis and the Struggle for dzilnchaasi'an (Mount Graham)." *NAIS: Journal of the Native American and Indigenous Studies Association* 1 (2): 151–75.

Hilden, Patricia Penn, and Leece M. Lee. 2010. "Indigenous Feminism: The Project." In *Indigenous Women and Feminism: Politics, Activism, Culture*, edited by Cheryl Suzack, Shari M. Huhndorf, Jeanne Perreault and Jean Barman, 56–77. Vancouver: University of British Columbia Press.

Honor the Earth. 2015a. "Honor the Earth." Accessed January 21, 2015. http://www.honorearth.org/.

———. 2015b. "Keystone XL." Accessed January 21, 2015. http://www.honorearth.org/keystone_xl.

hooks, bell. 2015. *Feminism Is for Everybody*. 2nd ed. New York: Routledge.

Hunn, Eugene S., and James Selam and Family. 1990. *Nch'i-Wána "The Big River": Mid-Columbia Indians and Their Land*. Seattle: University of Washington Press.

Indian Country Today Media Network. 2014. "Yakama Fight to Protect Fishing Sites From Coal Train Terminals." Indian Country Today Media Network. Last Modified May 21, 2014. Accessed September 3, 2014. http://indiancountrytodaymedianetwork.com/2014/05/21/yakama-come-out-swinging-against-coal-train-terminals-154970.

Jacob, Michelle M. 2008. "This Path Will Heal Our People: Healing the Soul Wound of Diabetes." In *Religion and Healing in Native America: Pathways for Renewal*, edited by Suzanne J. Crawford O'Brien, 43–62. Westport, CT: Praeger Publishers.

———. 2010a. "Claiming Health and Culture as Human Rights: Yakama Feminism in Daily Practice." *International Feminist Journal of Politics* 12 (3/4): 361–80.

———. 2010b. "Ethnography, Memory, and Culture: Healing the Soul Wound of Technological Disaster." In *How Ethnically Marginalized Americans Cope with Catastrophic Disasters*, edited by Jason S. Rivera and DeMond S. Miller, 37–49. Lewiston, ME: The Edwin Mellen Press.

———. 2013. *Yakama Rising: Indigenous Cultural Revitalization, Activism, and Healing*. Tucson: University of Arizona Press.

Jacob, Michelle M., and Wynona M Peters. 2011. "The Proper Way to Advance the Indian: Race and Gender Hierarchies in Early Yakima Newspapers." *Wicazo Sa Review* 27 (1): 39–55.

Jenkins, David, Joanne Bauer, Scott Bruton, Diane Austin, and Thomas McGuire. 2006. "Two Faces of American Environmentalism." In *Forging Environmentalism: Justice, Livelihood, and Contested Environments*, edited by Joanne Bauer, 262–326. Armonk, NY: M.E. Sharpe, Inc.

Johnson, Jan, Renee Holt, and Angela Picard. 2014. "Nimíipuu Nation Resistance to Tar Sands 'Megaloads': A New Chapter in an Old Story." American Indian Studies Association 15th Annual Meeting, Tempe, AZ, February 6, 2014.

Jolivétte, Andrew. 2006. *Cultural Representation in Native America*. Lanham, MD: AltaMira Press.

Koven, Suzanne. 2011. "Book Review: A nurse finds her real voice in lyrical memoir." Globe Newspaper Company. Last Modified July 25, 2011. Accessed February 2, 2015. http://www.boston.com/ae/books/articles/2011/07/25/in_memoir_one_nurses _life_mary_jane_nealon_finds_her_voice/.

LaDuke, Winona. 2005. *Recovering the Sacred*. Boston: South End Press.

———. 2014. "The New Indian Wars Coming to Rice Lake." *Indian Country Today*, June 27, 2014. http://indiancountrytodaymedianetwork.com/2014/06/27/new -indian-wars-coming-rice-lake-155522.

Lake Superior Binantional Forum. 2014. "Celebrate Lake Superior Day!" Sigurd Olson Environmental Institute Northland College. Accessed August 25, 2015. http:// www.superiorforum.org/outreach-2/lake-superior-day.

LaMore, Edward C., O.P. 1932. *The Lily of the Mohawks (Kateri Tekakwitha): An Historical Romance Drama of the American Indian*. Washington, DC: Dominicana.

Langdon, Stephen J. 2007. "Sustaining a Relationship." In *Native Americans and the Environment*, edited by Michael E. Harkin, 233–73. Lincoln: University of Nebraska Press.

Lee, Lloyd. 2014. Introduction. In *Diné Perspectives: Revitalizing and Reclaiming Navajo Thought*, edited by Lloyd Lee, 3–13. Tucson: University of Arizona Press.

Liao, Youlian, David Bang, Shannon Cosgrove, Rick Dulin, Zachery Harris, Alexandria Stewart, April Taylor, Shannon White, Graydon Yatabe, Leandris Liburd, and Wayne Giles. 2011. "Surveillance of Health Status in Minority Communities—

Racial and Ethnic Approaches to Community Health Across the U.S. (REACH U.S.) Risk Factor Survey, United States, 2009." (1545–8636 (Electronic)).

Lifsher, Marc. 2015. "Fracking Data." *Los Angeles Times*, February 2, 2015, A10.

Long-Garcia, J.D. 2011. "Native American sister develops institute to serve her people Sister Clissene Lewis of Arizona understands cultural challenges of community." *Our Sunday Visitor*. Accessed September 16, 2014.

Lugones, María. 2010. "Toward a Decolonial Feminism." *Hypatia* 25 (4): 742–59. doi: 10.1111/j.1527–2001.2010.01137.x.

McGhee, Gerry, Glenn R. Marland, and Jacqueline M. Atkinson. 2007. "Grounded Theory Research: Literature Reviewing and Reflexivity." *Journal of Advanced Nursing*. 60 (3): 334–42.

Marcel, Janet. 2015. "Father Roch R. Naquin." Diocese of Houma-Thibodaux. Accessed November 12, 2015. http://htdiocese.dashbee.com/blog/father-roch-r-naquin.

Merculieff, Larry, and Libby Roderick. 2013. *Stop Talking: Indigenous Ways of Teaching and Learning and Difficult Dialogues in Higher Education*. Anchorage: University of Alaska Press.

Middleton, Beth Rose. 2001. *Trust in the Land: New Directions in Tribal Conservation*. Tucson: University of Arizona Press.

Mihesuah, Devon Abbott, and Angela Cavender Wilson, eds. 2004. *Indigenizing the Academy: Transforming Scholarship and Empowering Communities*. Lincoln: University of Nebraska Press.

Million, Dian. 2009. "Felt Theory: An Indigenous Feminist Approach to Affect and History." *Wicazo Sa Review* 24 (2): 53–76.

———. 2013. *Therapeutic Nations: Healing in an Age of Indigenous Human Rights*, Critical Issues in Indigenous Studies. Tucson: University of Arizona Press.

———. 2014. "There is a River in Me." In *Theorizing Native Studies*, edited by Audra Simpson and Andrea Smith, 31–42. Durham, NC: Duke University Press.

Misleh, Dan. 2015. "Highlights of Pope Francis's Encyclical Letter on Ecology." Catholic Climate Covenant. Accessed June 19, 2015. http://www.sandiego.edu/cctc/documents/Catholic+Climate+Covenant+encyclical+excerpts1.pdf.

Mitchell, Kateri. 1996. "Program Development and Native American Catechesis." In *Native and Christian: Indigenous Voices on Religious Identity in the United States and Canada*, edited by James Treat, 170–77. New York: Routledge.

———. 2012. "From the Desk of the Tekakwitha Conference Executive Director." In *Native Footsteps: Along the Path of Saint Kateri Tekakwitha*, edited by

Mark G. Thiel and Christopher Vecsey, 129–30. Milwaukee: Marquette University Press.

Montreuil, Brandi N. 2015. "Long time priest to Tulalip made honorary tribal member." *Tulalip News.* Accessed November 12, 2015. http://www.tulalipnews.com /wp/2015/07/15/long-time-priest-to-tulalip-made-honorary-tribal-member/.

Nealon, Mary Jane. 2011. *Beautiful Unbroken: One Nurse's Life.* Minneapolis, MN: Graywolf Press.

Newcomb, Steven T. 2008. *Pagans in the Promised Land: Decoding the Doctrine of Christian Discovery.* Golden, CO: Fulcrum Publishing.

Nippert, Bernadette, Brenda Nippert, and George Nippert. 2012. *My Soul Magnifies the Greatness of the Lord: Saint Kateri Tekakwitha.* Carlisle, PA: Joseph's Heartprint.

Norgaard, Kari Marie. 2011. *Living in Denial: Climate Change, Emotions, and Everyday Life.* Cambridge, MA: MIT Press.

O'Connell, J., R. Yi, C. Wilson, S. M. Manson, and K. J. Acton. 2010. "Racial disparities in health status: a comparison of the morbidity among American Indian and U.S. adults with diabetes." *Diabetes Care* 33 (7): 1463–70. doi: dc09–1652 [pii] 10.2337/dc09–1652 [doi].

O'Leary, Michael. 2014. "Yakama Nation to Coal: And Stay Out." BlueOregon. Accessed September 3, 2014. http://www.blueoregon.com/2014/08/yakama-nation -coal-and-stay-out/.

Palmer, Vera B. 2014. "The Devil in the Details: Controverting an American Indian Conversion Narrative." In *Theorizing Native Studies*, edited by Audra Simpson and Andrea Smith, 266–96. Durham, NC: Duke University Press.

Pope Benedict XVI. 2009. "If You Want to Cultivate Peace, Protect Creation." Libreria Editrice Vaticana. Accessed January 28, 2015. http://www.vatican.va/holy _father/benedict_xvi/messages/peace/documents/hf_ben-xvi_mes_20091208 _xliii-world-day-peace_en.html

Pope Francis. 2015. "Encyclical Letter: Laudato Si': On Care for Our Common Home." Libreria Editrice Vaticana. Accessed June 18, 2015. http://w2.vatican.va/content /francesco/en/encyclicals/documents/papa-francesco_20150524_enciclica-laudato -si.html

Porter, Joy. 2012. *Land and Spirit in Native America.* Santa Barbara, CA: Praeger.

———. *Native American Environmentalism: Land, Spirit, and the Idea of Wilderness.* Lincoln: University of Nebraska Press.

Portman, Tarrell A. A., and Michael T. Garrett. 2006. "Native American Healing Traditions." *International Journal of Disability, Development and Education* 53 (4): 453–69.

Sander-Palmer, Sharon. 2013. "Indigenous Women Walking Entire Mississippi River to Raise Awareness of Water Pollution's Impact. *Daily Gate City*. Accessed September 16, 2014.

Sargent, Daniel. 1936. *Catherine Tekakwitha*. New York: Longmans, Green and Co.

Shepherd, Jeffrey P. 2010. *We Are an Indian Nation: A History of the Hualapai People*, First Peoples: New Directions in Indigenous Studies. Tucson: University of Arizona Press.

Sherman, Rev. Edward. 2007. *Tekakwitha: Holy Native, Mohawk Virgin, 1656–80*. Grand Forks, ND: Fine Print of Grand Forks, Inc.

Shoemaker, Nancy. 1995. "Kateri Tekakwitha's Tortuous Path to Sainthood." In *Negotiators of Change: Historical Perspectives on Native American Women*, edited by Nancy Shoemaker, 49–71. New York: Routledge.

Sierra Club—Wisconsin John Muir Chapter. 2015. "Blocking Destructive Mining." Accessed November 10, 2015. http://www.sierraclub.org/wisconsin/issues/mining.

Silko, Leslie Marmon. 1981. *Storyteller*. New York: Arcade Pub.: Little, Brown and Company.

Simonson, Mike. 2014. "Wisconsin Tribes Refuse to Sit on State Mining Impact Board." Wisconsin Public Radio. Last Modified August 6, 2014. Accessed September 3, 2014. http://www.wpr.org/wisconsin-tribes-refuse-sit-state-mining-impact -board.

Smith, Andrea. 2003. "Not an Indian Tradition: The Sexual Colonization of Native Peoples." *Hypatia* 18 (2): 70–85. doi: 10.1111/j.1527–2001.2003.tb00802.x.

———. 2005a. *Conquest*. Boston: South End Press.

———. 2005b. "Native American Feminism, Sovereignty, and Social Change." *Feminist Studies* 31 (1): 116–32.

———. 2006. "Heteropatriarchy and the Three Pillars of White Supremacy." In *Color of Violence: The Incite! Anthology*, edited by Incite! Women of Color Against Violence, 66–78. Cambridge, MA: South End Press.

———. 2008. *Native Americans and the Christian Right*. Durham, NC: Duke University Press.

———. 2010. "Decolonization in Unexpected Places: Native Evangelicalism and the Rearticulation of Mission." *American Quarterly* 62 (3): 569–90.

———. 2014. "Native Studies at the Horizon of Death." In *Theorizing Native Studies*, edited by Audra Simpson and Andrea Smith, 207–34. Durham, NC: Duke University Press.

Smith, Justine. 1996. "Custer Rides Again—This Time on the Exxon Valdez." In *Defending Mother Earth: Native American Perspectives on Environmental Justice*, edited by Jace Weaver, 59–71. Maryknoll, NY: Orbis Books.

Smith, Linda Tuhiwai. 2012. *Decolonizing Methodologies: Research and Indigenous Peoples*. 2nd ed. London: Zed Books.

State of Wisconsin. 2015. "Gogebic Taconite, LLC, potential mining project." Wisconsin Department of Natural Resources. Accessed November 13, 2015. http://dnr.wi.gov/topic/Mines/Gogebic.html.

Stevens, Stan. 1997. Introduction. In *Conservation Through Cultural Survival: Indigenous Peoples and Protected Areas*, edited by Stan Stevens, 1–7. Washington, DC: Island Press.

———. 2014. "Indigenous Peoples, Biocultural Diversity, and Protected Areas." In *Indigenous Peoples, National Parks, and Protected Areas: A New Paradigm Linking Conservation, Culture, and Rights*, edited by Stan Stevens, 3–46. Tucson: University of Arizona Press.

Strauss, Anselm, and Juliet Corbin. 1990. *Basics of Qualitative Research: Grounded Theory Procedures and Techniques*. Newbury Park, CA: Sage Publications.

Tarango, Angela. 2014. *Choosing the Jesus Way: Native American Pentecostals and the Fight For the Indigenous Principle*. Chapel Hill: University of North Carolina Press.

Thiel, Mark G. 2012. "Jake Finkbonner and the Miracle at Seattle Children's Hospital." In *Native Footsteps: Along the Path of Saint Kateri Tekakwitha*, edited by Mark G. Thiel and Christopher Vecsey, 121–27. Milwaukee, WI: Marquette University Press.

Thiel, Mark G., and Christopher Vecsey, eds. 2012. *Native Footsteps: Along the Path of Saint Kateri Tekakwitha*. Milwaukee, WI: Marquette University Press.

Tinker, George E. 1993. *Missionary Conquest: The Gospel and Native American Cultural Genocide*. Minneapolis, MN: Fortress Press.

———. 2004. *Spirit and Resistance: Political Theology and American Indian Liberation*. Minneapolis, MN: Fortress Press.

Tinker, Tink. 2014. "Redskin, Tanned Hide: A Book of Christian History Bound in the Flayed Skin of an American Indian: The Colonial Romance, Christian Denial and the Cleansing of a Christian School of Theology." *Journal of Race, Ethnicity, and Religion* 5 (9): 1–43.

Treat, James, ed. 1996. *Native and Christian: Indigenous Voices on Religious Identity in the United States and Canada*. New York: Routledge.

Tuck, Eve, and Wayne Yang. 2012. "Decolonization Is Not a Metaphor." *Decolonization: Indigeneity, Education and Society* 1 (1): 1–40.

Twohy, Patrick J. 2009. *Finding a Way Home: Indian and Catholic Spiritual Paths of the Plateau Tribes*. Spokane, WA: Aspenels Printing.

U.S. Department of Commerce. 2013. "Alcoa Aluminum Factories Settle $19.4 Million for Pollution of St. Lawrence River Watershed, Most Will Fund Restoration of Tribal Culture, Recreational Fishing, and Habitat." Last Modified June 17, 2014. Accessed June 19, 2014. http://response.restoration.noaa.gov/about/media/alcoa-aluminum-factories-settle-194-million-pollution-st-lawrence-river-watershed-most-w.

Uebelacker, Morris L. 1984. *Time Ball: A Story of the Yakima People and the Land*. Yakama, WA: The Yakama Nation.

University of Washington Digital Collections. "American Indians of the Pacific Northwest Collection." University of Washington Libraries. Accessed January 21, 2015. http://content.lib.washington.edu/aipnw/early_reminiscences_speech.html.

Vecsey, Christopher. 2012. Introduction. In *Native Footsteps: Along the Path of Saint Kateri Tekakwitha*, edited by Mark G. Thiel and Christopher Vecsey, 13–36. Milwaukee, WI: Marquette University Press.

Vicenti Carpio, Myla. 2011. *Indigenous Albuquerque*. Lubbock: Texas Tech University Press.

Walker, Richard. 2012. "Yakama Elder Talks About Kateri's Canonization and What It Means to Native Catholics." *Native Strength*. Last Modified November 2, 2012. Accessed June 20, 2014. http://nativestrength.com/2012/11/02/yakama-elder-talks-about-kateris-canonization-and-what-it-means-to-native-catholics/.

Weiser, Francis X. 1971. *Kateri Tekakwitha*. Montreal: The Kateri Center, Caughnawaga.

Whatoname, Wilfred, Sr. 2010. "Foreword." In *We Are an Indian Nation: A History of the Hualapai People*, edited by Jeffrey P. Shepherd, xiii–xiv. Tucson: University of Arizona Press.

Wilson, Shawn. 2008. *Research Is Ceremony: Indigenous Research Methods*. Halifax, Nova Scotia: Fernwood Publishing.

Wojtanik, Robin. 2011. "'Lily of the Mohawks' to Be Named a Saint, Yakima Catholics 'Rejoicing.'" KIMA TV. Accessed December 20, 2011. http://www.kimatv.com/news/local/Lily-of-the-Mohawks-to-be-named-a-saint-by-Catholic-church-135904983.html.

Women's Nibi Conversation Group. 2013. "Women's Nibi Conversation Gathering Notes." March 15, 2013.

Yakima Indian Nation Tribal Council. 1977. *The Land of the Yakimas*, edited by Robert E. Pace and Kamiakin Research Institute. Toppenish, WA: Yakima Indian Nation.

Zucchino, David. 2015. "Duke Energy Fined Millions." *Los Angeles Times*, May 15, 2015, A8.

Index

Vatican: dispute over Mt. Graham, 125; Saint Kateri's canonization and, 4*f*, 5, 8, 11, 13*f*, 15, 21, 25, 33, 117, 129

Vecsey, Christopher, 5–6

vestments, Saint Kateri-themed, 26, 127, 128, 130, 133, 140, 154

violence: effect upon Saint Kateri, 10, 116, 141; land dispossession and, 56, 63; "unspeakable" forms of, 111, 113, 118, 123, 141, 153. *See also* colonialism; gender violence

virgin forests, compared to virgin Mohawk maiden, 119–24

Walker, Scott, 58

Wallowa Valley, 63

Wapato Indian Club, 86

Wapato Middle School, 86

waste treatment centers, 59

water (nibi), 54–55, 60, 66; Ginibiimanaan poster, 40, 59, 59*n*; towers, 59; Women's Nibi Conversation, 59–60

Water Walks and Water Walkers, 34, 40–41, 59, 60, 69–70, 78; at University of San Diego, 143–46, 146*f*, 147, 150, 158

Waykáanash (salmon), 61, 62*f*, 63, 87

Weiser, Francis X., 12, 22–23

"What Can I Hope to Be for My People" (prayer), 77

Whatoname, Wilfred, Sr., 153

White Swan, Washington. *See* Yakama Nation and Reservation

Wiggins, Mike, 57, 58

wildfires, 145

wildlife, 46, 59, 145, 162*f*

Williams, Ray (Squi Qui), 99–102, 100*f*, 151

Wilson, Shawn, 11–12

World Day of Peace 2010, 50

Wright, John Cardinal, 22

Yakama Nation and Reservation, 34, 73–75, 89, 109; author as member of, 11; fishing and gathering rights, 60–61, 62*f*, 63; importance of Saint Kateri to, 12, 21, 35, 133–34, 134*f*, 135; Saint Mary's Church, 61, 62*f*, 84–89; Tekakwitha Conference attendees, 84*f*; Yakama Healthy Heart Community Track Meet, 74, 88; Yakama Healthy Heart Program, 74, 88

About the Author

Michelle M. Jacob (Yakama) is associate professor of education studies and director of the Sapsikʷatá (Teacher) Education Program at the University of Oregon. She previously served as the founding director of the Center for Native Health and Culture at Heritage University on the Yakama Reservation, and as professor of ethnic studies at the University of San Diego. Michelle engages in scholarly and activist work that seeks to understand and work toward a holistic sense of health and well-being within Indigenous communities. Dr. Jacob's first book, *Yakama Rising: Indigenous Cultural Revitalization, Activism, and Healing*, was published by the University of Arizona Press as part of the First Peoples: New Directions in Indigenous Studies Series.

About the Cover

The cover features a turtle in honor of Kateri Tekakwitha's clan. This particular turtle image is used with permission from the Pendleton Woolen Mills, who featured this image on their "Creation Turtle Blanket," which recognizes the Iroquois Confederacy and honors the Iroquois Creation Story of how the world was created on a turtle's shell. The turtle symbolizes strength and healing, and continues to be a source of inspiration for many Indigenous peoples, including Sister Kateri Mitchell, Akwesasne Mohawk elder and executive director of the National Tekakwitha Conference, and Dr. Gayle Skawen:nio Morse (Akwesasne Mohawk), both of whom helped advise the author in choosing a culturally respectful cover design for this book.